"I suspect Pope Francis would be pr 's
to his message. It's the kind of thing "
— James Lee Bur it

"If you are looking for a book to gi :-
ing to live the social teachings of the Catholic faith, I can't think of a better
work of recent years than *What Would Pope Francis Do?* Tales from the lives
of saints and an introduction to the basics of Jesuit spirituality round out this
entertaining and highly accessible narrative."
— Dawn Eden, author and theologian

"*What Would Pope Francis Do?* is a health-giving blend of personal anecdote,
Jesuit spirituality, and papal teaching, deftly packing anecdote and insight
into its well-crafted pages. For anyone who wants to accept Pope Francis's
invitation to live closer to Jesus, Salai is the perfect travel companion: witty,
wise, and challenging."
— Austen Ivereigh, author of *The Great Reformer:*
Francis and the Making of a Radical Pope

"As a woman who has sheltered homeless unwed mothers so they can give
the gift of life to their precious pre-born children, I found each chapter to be
a workshop of knowledge and heavenly inspiration. I have read several books
on the life of Pope Francis but none as relevant and inspirational to the challenges young people and their advisers face."
— Kathy DiFiore, founder of Several Sources Shelters

"I recommend this book highly. Forget the controversies that follow our first
pope from South America and you'll understand that Pope Francis above all
is eager to bring all Christians together so they may bring all mankind into
the fold."
— Fr. C. John McCloskey, spiritual director and author

"Reading through *What Would Pope Francis Do?*, one can't help but be in-
spired to love deeper, to be more merciful, to give more of oneself, and to let
Christ shine through."
— Kristan Hawkins, president of Students for Life of America

"Sean Salai, S.J., uses fascinating examples from history, Scripture, and personal experience to illuminate the teachings of Pope Francis in a way that
perhaps only a fellow Jesuit could do. This book left me wanting to be a
better person."
— Ronald J. Rychlak, professor of law and
author of *Hitler, the War, and the Pope*

"A book bringing together the various practical things we find in Pope Francis, things that help explain why we are as we are, is most welcome. Salai senses the pastoral side of our Argentine Holy Father."

— Fr. James V. Schall, S.J., professor emeritus,
Georgetown University

"This marvelous little book is filled with moving anecdotes and life lessons on how to live out the Gospel of Joy from one Jesuit to another — to you and me."

— Gus Lloyd, apologist and host of *Seize the Day*
on Sirius XM's The Catholic Channel

"In compelling, fast-paced narrative, Salai unpacks *The Joy of the Gospel*, revealing Pope Francis's passionate plan for evangelization to the marginalized. The result is an empowering tapestry that demands Gospel action everywhere and for everyone."

— Dale Recinella, Florida death row chaplain and author

"Through his clear and compelling analysis, Salai opens a window into the heart of Pope Francis, giving us a glimpse into that spiritual wellspring from which the Holy Father speaks of the tenderness of God's love and the need for all believers to bring that love to a waiting world. I highly recommend this book to all who wish to answer the call of Pope Francis to become joyful agents of mercy in mission."

— Bishop Frank Caggiano, Diocese of Bridgeport

"With a lively and engaging narrative style, Salai takes us on a pilgrimage through the thinking and spirituality of Pope Francis and then invites us to apply these principles in our own lives as the disciples of Jesus Christ."

— Mother Agnes Mary Donovan, S.V.,
Superior General of the Sisters of Life

"Sean Salai, S.J., proves an excellent companion and guide as we learn how to read our first Jesuit pope and to become familiar with the spirituality that has formed him. *What Would Pope Francis Do?* will have a strong, dare I say magnetic, impact on many, and I particularly recommend it for students."

— Elizabeth Scalia, writer and English-language editor
of the international Catholic website Aleteia.org

What Would Pope Francis Do?

Bringing the Good News to People in Need

What Would
POPE
Francis
Do?

BRINGING THE
GOOD NEWS TO
PEOPLE IN NEED

Sean Salai, S.J.

Our Sunday Visitor Publishing Division
Our Sunday Visitor, Inc.
Huntington, Indiana 46750

Imprimi Potest:
Very Rev. Ronald A. Mercier, S.J., Provincial
U.S.A. Central and Southern Province of the Society of Jesus

Imprimatur:
✠ Most Rev. Michael C. Barber, S.J.
Bishop of Oakland
September 10, 2015

The *Imprimi Potest* and *Imprimatur* are declarations that a work is free from doctrinal or moral error. It is not implied that those who have granted the *Imprimi Potest* and *Imprimatur* agree with the contents, opinions, or statements expressed.

Parts of chapter 5 and the conclusion in this book are based on essay material that originally appeared online in *America*, the national Catholic review.

Scripture texts in this work are taken from the *New American Bible, revised edition* © 2010, 1991, 1986, 1970 Confraternity of Christian Doctrine, Washington, D.C., and are used by permission of the copyright owner. All rights reserved. No part of the *New American Bible* may be reproduced in any form without permission in writing from the copyright owner.

Excerpts from the *Catechism of the Catholic Church, Second Edition*, for use in the United States of America, copyright © 1994 and 1997, United States Catholic Conference — Libreria Editrice Vaticana. Used by permission. All rights reserved.

Quotations from papal and other Vatican-generated documents available on vatican.va are copyright © Libreria Editrice Vaticana.

Every reasonable effort has been made to determine copyright holders of excerpted materials and to secure permissions as needed. If any copyrighted materials have been inadvertently used in this work without proper credit being given in one form or another, please notify Our Sunday Visitor in writing so that future printings of this work may be corrected accordingly.

Copyright © 2016 by the U.S.A. Central and Southern Province of the Society of Jesus. Published 2016.

20 19 18 17 16   1 2 3 4 5 6 7 8 9

All rights reserved. With the exception of short excerpts for critical reviews, no part of this work may be reproduced or transmitted in any form or by any means whatsoever without permission from the publisher. For more information, visit: www.osv.com/permissions.

Our Sunday Visitor Publishing Division, Our Sunday Visitor, Inc., 200 Noll Plaza, Huntington, IN 46750; 1-800-348-2440.

ISBN: 978-1-61278-960-6 (Inventory No. T1727)
eISBN: 978-1-61278-962-0
LCCN: 2015959973

Cover design: Amanda Falk
Cover images: iStock and Shutterstock

PRINTED IN THE UNITED STATES OF AMERICA

✠ Ad Majorem Dei Gloriam ✠

Contents

JOY

We do well to keep in mind the early Christians and our many brothers and sisters throughout history who were filled with joy, unflagging courage and zeal in proclaiming the Gospel. (Evangelii Gaudium *263*)

"What if the next pope is a Jesuit?"

With an impatient sigh, I turned from the projector screen to identify the fifteen-year-old student who had asked me this question.

It was March 2013. Blue skies and 72 degrees of Florida sunshine awaited us outside the windows of our darkened classroom in Tampa. I, the all-knowing Jesuit theology teacher, did not want to spend much time speculating about a "Jesuit pope" during our lesson on the upcoming papal conclave. I wanted a cup of coffee.

After all, I had four more sections of freshman boys to teach that day at Jesuit High School, and we hadn't even gotten to the white smoke. At the rate we were going, our next pope might be elected before we learned how to count the votes.

Maybe that explains why, rather than giving a nuanced answer, I loaded my intellectual guns and aimed to stop the question in its tracks.

"That's not going to happen," I told the kid, using my most matter-of-fact teacher voice.

Bang. I felt pretty good about myself.

But the kid, one of my favorite students, quickly shot back: "Why not?"

I sighed again.

"It won't happen because we Jesuits take a vow to avoid positions of honor in the Catholic Church whenever possible. We don't become monsignors, and we don't become bishops unless the pope insists. And there's never been a Jesuit pope. St. Ignatius didn't want us messing around with that stuff."

As I gave this answer, I could hear in my head all of the wisecracks from the Jesuit rec room, reassuring me in my certainty. "Hell will freeze over before a Jesuit becomes pope." We've all heard that sort of thing before.

If a Jesuit cardinal wasn't seeking the papacy, but was following the Jesuit rule to avoid politicking, there was no reason for the other 114 cardinals to elect him. That was common sense. Right?

The Election

Yet my freshman theology student, who had a soft spot for underdogs, wasn't going to let me off the hook about the slim possibility that a Jesuit might become pope.

He spoke up again.

"Who are the Jesuit cardinals? I just want to know."

Softening to his curiosity, I clicked through the list of cardinals on my computer and pointed out an Asian Jesuit who was not attending the conclave due to illness. Then I pulled up the Vatican website's biography of Cardinal Jorge Mario Bergoglio, S.J., the only Jesuit cardinal who would actually be attending and voting for pope. He was archbishop of Buenos Aires, Argentina.

After glancing at Cardinal Bergoglio's photo and briefly reading some of his biography out loud, I told the class I was reasonably certain — as a fellow Jesuit — that this guy would *not* get elected.

My hopeful student, of course, was not so sure. He asked: "But what if it happens? What if he gets elected anyway?"

I just shrugged.

In my four remaining classes that day, I repeated this whole ritual, showing my freshmen a photo of the Jesuit cardinal and denying he would be elected pope.

According to the Gospels, St. Peter denied Jesus three times on one occasion. In five different class periods, I had denied that the Holy Spirit would ever pick a Jesuit to succeed St. Peter.

By the end of the school day, I felt pretty satisfied. We had covered the basics of papal conclaves, and I had put the "Jesuit pope" silliness to rest. Or so I thought.

A few days later, on March 13, we were watching the white smoke on a live feed in class when God decided not to heed my prediction.

"Habemus papam!"

Twenty-five teenage boys turned to stare at me in shock as Cardinal Bergoglio walked to the edge of a balcony in St. Peter's Square, dressed in white as the newly elected Pope Francis.

Television cameras from Tampa's FOX and ABC news affiliates, invited to record our school's on-the-spot reaction to the announcement of a new pope, captured our joyful surprise in the theology classrooms as students erupted in cheers. They also interviewed our students in the hallway after Francis appeared on the balcony.

Asked his thoughts about having a Latin American pope for the first time in history, one of my students, whose great-uncle was a cardinal in the Dominican Republic, told ABC Action News: "I guess he's reppin' for us."

I was also interviewed by ABC, and I admitted that my own reaction was "utter disbelief."

I, like nearly every other Jesuit in the world, had been wrong on this one. Pigs were flying on the winds of the Holy Spirit. Hell had frozen over and left me shivering, dressed in short sleeves.

To his credit, the new pope on the balcony looked just as surprised as we did. After waving shyly and saying a few words of greeting, he bowed his head and asked the crowd in St. Peter's Square to pray for him. It was a profound moment of silence that our students shared with the rest of the world through the classroom projector screens.

As chapel bells rang out across campus, the school president soon announced our first Jesuit pope over the intercom for students and faculty who hadn't been watching it live. In my classroom, the boys snapped photos of the new pope on screen with their iPhones and sent them to family members.

The next several hours became a blur.

By 10:00 that night, I was out with another Jesuit retrieving liturgical torches and framing a photo of Pope Francis for a solemn Eucharistic benediction in our chapel the next morning.

We found an image of Pope Francis's first appearance on the Internet and had it blown up into portrait-sized prints at Kinko's. Then we inserted this image into an old frame, laying it flat over a portrait of Pope Emeritus Benedict XVI. Another copy of the print was soon hanging in my classroom, astounding my students that I had obtained one within hours of the papal election.

Two more television news crews, coming from our local NBC and CBS affiliates, descended in the morning to film our school's solemn benediction of thanksgiving for the election of Pope Francis. Yellow and white papal bunting hung down from above the chapel doors for benediction, with 750 students and faculty erupting in applause, shouts, and whistles before incense from two thuribles filled the space.

Fr. Richard C. Hermes, S.J., the school president, inspired this ovation with a memorable line before the liturgy. Stepping up to the pulpit, he declared: "Well, I'm not yet fifty, and I've seen snow in New Orleans on Christmas day, I've ridden on a camel in the deserts of Egypt, and now I've seen a Jesuit elected pope!"

Meanwhile, Francis wasn't holding back from setting the tone of his papacy. He had already signaled that he would be the pope of the marginalized, calling on Catholics by his words and deeds to go out to the peripheries of society as missionaries of God's love.

The new pontiff delivered this message with an informal and simple personal style. He mingled with ordinary people as he pleased, confusing Vatican security teams. Personally austere, he wore an unadorned white cassock over his clerical black pants and black shoes, confounding papal fashionistas.

Francis also renounced the papal apartments in the Vatican's apostolic palace, taking up residence in a small room at the Santa Marta guesthouse. Checking out of the room where he had stayed during the conclave, he paid his own bill with a credit card.

Asked later about this decision, he said he knew with one look that he couldn't stay in the papal apartments by himself. He needed to live around people, because, as he said, it was good for his "physical health."

International media jumped on every detail of the Argentinian pope's first appearances, including the selection of St. Francis of Assisi — the saint of the poor — as his namesake. Not only was he the first pope from the Americas and the first Jesuit pope, but he was also the first to take the name of St. Francis, the medieval playboy-turned-beggar who founded the religious order we know as the Franciscans.

News agencies throughout the world were soon airing a St. Francis-like photo of Cardinal Bergoglio riding the subway in Buenos Aires during his time as archbishop. In this photo he wears a simple black raincoat, closed around the neck, and he looks like everyone else on the train.

Pope Francis further endeared himself to world opinion by displaying a ready sense of humor in his first audience with journalists at the Vatican on March 16, 2013. Noting that Pope Clement XIV had suppressed his Jesuit order in 1773, plunging the Society of Jesus into near-extinction until its universal restoration in 1814, Francis joked that he had considered taking the papal name "Clement XV."

"That way you can take revenge on Clement XIV for suppressing the Society of Jesus," Francis reported one cardinal telling him after the election.

But it wasn't just Francis's public persona that won people's hearts. The world soon discovered that there was substance behind the popular style of this man who, not long before his election as pope, had submitted his age-mandated resignation as archbishop and started planning his retirement.

A Missionary Church

Through bold gestures, Francis soon began to share the weightier message of his papacy, challenging Catholics to greater depths of belief and practice.

Within three months of his election, the new pope finished and published an encyclical letter on faith (*Lumen Fidei*) started by his predecessor, Benedict XVI. He elevated third-world cardinals to positions of global leadership, launching efforts to reform the Vatican's bureaucracy. To get feedback on these efforts, he created an advisory commission of cardinals, appointing one of them (Cardinal George Pell of Australia) as his point man to oversee a financial overhaul of the scandal-plagued Vatican Bank.

In a touching gesture of respect, Francis even met with his predecessor at Castel Gandolfo, where the retired Benedict XVI prayed with him and briefed the Jesuit on his new job. The first pope to resign the Petrine ministry since Gregory XII in 1415, Benedict soon moved to a monastery on the Vatican grounds and became a familiar face at official functions during Francis's papacy.

But perhaps the fullest revelation of Francis's vision for the Catholic Church came in November 2013, when he wrote the apostolic exhortation *Evangelii Gaudium* (*The Joy of the Gospel*) as a blueprint for Catholics on how to preach the Gospel in today's world. In this document, Francis writes:

> Each Christian and every community must discern the path that the Lord points out, but all of us are asked to obey his call to go forth from our own comfort zone in order to reach all the "peripheries" in need of the light of the Gospel. (*Evangelii Gaudium* 20)

To be Catholic, then, is to be always on mission — a worldwide mission of evangelization to the peripheries or margins of our society, where people are most in need of Gospel joy.

Rather than be "sourpusses," as the pope puts it elsewhere in the document, God invites us to be joyful in sharing his "good news" (the meaning of the word "gospel") with others. And God asks us to work together with other Christians, responding to the call of our common baptism, in doing so.

While this message is hardly new to Catholicism, Pope Francis's background gives it a distinctive flavor and urgency. As a Jesuit, Francis comes from a religious order that is always on mission, regardless of whether that mission occurs in one's own backyard or on the other side of the globe. And a spirit of Christ-centered discernment shapes this missionary perspective on being Catholic: Francis asks us, as individuals and as communities, to pray before we act.

So then what does it mean for *all* believers to "go forth from our own comfort zone" as missionaries to the margins? Whom do we find there? And what must we do to bring Christ's love to the margins as a missionary church?

Rather than give blanket answers to these questions, Francis invites Christians to discern where the Lord is leading us. To get answers, we must take our questions to God in prayer and listen for his voice, asking for the grace to know God's will and to do it in our lives. We must see, judge, and act on the Lord's call in the context of our shared baptismal mission.

Francis, emphasizing that divine love precedes and enables our response of human love, adds that going to the margins requires Christians to first be rooted in a deeply felt knowledge of Christ's personal love for each of us:

> An evangelizing community knows that the Lord has taken the initiative, he has loved us first (cf. 1 Jn 4:19), and therefore we can move forward, boldly take the initiative, go out to others, seek those who have fallen away, stand at the crossroads and welcome the outcast. (*Evangelii Gaudium* 24)

So the margins include those who have fallen away and are outcast. But we Christians, as individuals and as an evangelizing community, must get our own house in order before we can bring real healing to our world. Above all else, our work must be rooted in a joyful conviction of Christ's love for us that is genuine and spontaneous rather than merely dutiful.

In other words, each of us is called to a deep personal relationship with Jesus Christ.

As bishop and as pope, Francis has been particularly close to evangelical Christians and to charismatic Catholics on this all-important framework for evangelization. Once we feel secure in our conviction of Christ's love for us, the pope says we will find ourselves called to move outward — not further inward — to share that love with people on the margins in a way that makes a difference. We will respond to God's freely offered love by loving others freely.

Accordingly, while the starting point is internal, we cannot remain centered on ourselves. Even monks pray for others more than for themselves. To inspire others with the good news, our personal experience of Christ's love must yield fruit in concrete action, inspiring us to love others through our deeds more than through our words.

In a September 2013 interview with Jesuit journals from around the world, published in multiple languages, Francis expressed this idea by saying he longed for the Catholic Church to be a "field hospital" of God's love and mercy to people in need. As for his own role in steering the barque of Peter, the pope described himself frankly as a sinner in need of God's mercy, just like anyone else.

Not only in this interview, but throughout his papacy, Francis has called on believers to pray for the grace to get out of our pews and shake things up by making a joyful noise. Rather than wait for people to come to our parishes, we need to go outside and meet them where they are.

Our mission to the margins is not merely a job for ordained shepherds, whom Francis exhorted in an early homily to "smell like the sheep," but for all of us. Francis reminds us that God calls all believers universally, in the waters of baptism, to be disciples who are priests, prophets, and kings — in other words, self-giving leaders who act boldly to build a better world.

Looking at chapter 5 of *The Joy of the Gospel*, I believe we may discern the essence of Francis's message in six themes that evoke his vision for a church of missionaries sent to the margins:

- Longing. The longing for God is innate in everyone — this
  is what we were made for, to be in relationship with God.

- Closeness. We must be close to people's lives: "enter fully into the fabric of society"; step away from "personal or
  communal niches which shelter us from the maelstrom of
  human misfortune"; lead "wonderfully complicated lives."

- Dignity. Every person is worthy of our giving.

- Weariness. When we go to the margins, we must be honest about how it affects us, transforming our fatigue into
  an ever-deepening outreach that is energizing and compassionate.

- Tenderness. Francis uses this word a lot. He talks about
  how it characterizes his interactions with others, and about
  how it might characterize ours.

- Mary. The Mother of Evangelization remains an ever-pres-
  ent model of discipleship.

Throughout the next six chapters of this book, I will follow these themes in reflecting on what it means for us to leave
our parishes and go out to the margins in imitation of Christ.
Then I will conclude with a few thoughts on the implications
of this message for courageous discipleship in the future.

With the visit of Pope Francis to the United States in
September 2015 for the World Meeting of Families, many
Americans have now had the chance to see the Holy Father in
person. We've heard his voice and read his words on going out
to the fringes of society as missionaries of Christ's love, even
when it means healing the brokenness of our own families in
a world of fast-changing values.

Again and again, Pope Francis urges all Christians: Go
be missionaries of Jesus Christ's love to people on the margins.

I hope this book will introduce readers to this key message in the teaching and life of Francis in a deeper way, inspir-

ing us to more profoundly embrace the call of Jesus in our lives.

Of course, answering that call will be challenging at times. Striving to follow it in our daily routines, we might find ourselves tempted to doubt that our good news will really change the world. We may feel too beaten down by life and too disillusioned by past experiences to believe in the reality of Gospel joy.

However, as I hope the stories in this book will show, nothing is impossible with God. Not even a Jesuit pope.

CHAPTER ONE

LONGING

The primary reason for evangelizing is the love of Jesus which we have received, the experience of salvation which urges us to ever greater love of him. What kind of love would not feel the need to speak of the beloved, to point him out, to make him known?

If we do not feel an intense desire to share this love, we need to pray insistently that he will once more touch our hearts. We need to implore his grace daily, asking him to open our cold hearts and shake up our lukewarm and superficial existence. (Evangelii Gaudium *264*)

A few months after the election of Pope Francis, my Jesuit High School students and I went to sleep hungry on a Brazilian beach, surrounded by three million people as the icy surf washed toward us.

We were spending a chilly July night on Copacabana Beach in Rio de Janeiro, waiting for Francis to celebrate Mass with us in the morning. It was the closing liturgy of World Youth Day and the Brazilian winter (June–August) was in full swing.

That night, July 27, we shivered in our sleeping bags. Earlier in the day, the sun had cooked us for hours with a withering heat. Florida felt very far away.

As temperatures fell steadily during the evening, it was tough to rest peacefully. Our students built little sand walls to block the wind and to keep the freezing ocean spray from blasting us. These walls also gave us an illusion of privacy: The entire 2.5-mile beach was crammed shoulder-to-shoulder with snoring pilgrims, tents, and camping gear.

Our sleep was marked by the taste of salt water, the sound of waves crashing rhythmically on the beach, and the feeling of cold sand digging into our backs. When we got hungry, we nibbled on a little canned tuna and dry snacks which organizers had handed out in boxes before police closed the beach.

To our dismay, the only thing less comfortable than the beach itself was the row of portable toilets lined up alongside it. With beach exits closed and nowhere else to go, organizers had vastly underestimated the number of pilgrims, and some of the facilities were overflowing. It wasn't sheep we smelled that night.

Francis, whose motorcade passed our group after he arrived by helicopter in the morning, celebrated Mass from an enormous platform, visible to us only through giant television screens spread out along the beach. We were at least two miles away from him.

One of our students, staking out a spot right next to the beachside road, found himself at the front of a cheering crowd as Francis drove by that morning.

When the papal motorcade paused briefly for Francis to wave at some beachfront apartment windows, where people leaned out to greet him, our student snapped a crystal-clear photograph of the pope with his digital camera. He was on cloud nine.

The Mass itself turned out to be a lively mix of Spanish, Portuguese, and Latin hymns — all set to joyful music that led the Brazilian pilgrims to dance.

While many of the guys in our group longed to receive Jesus in the Eucharist, or to at least be closer to Francis, the crowd was so big that most of us could not get anywhere near a communion station. Two of our students who hadn't eaten a hot meal in twelve hours were so tired that they simply slept through half of the liturgy, curled up in a fetal position.

In his homily, delivered in Spanish over loudspeakers, Francis summarized the week's festivities by asking us one last time to be missionaries of God's love. "Go be missionaries," he declared, echoing the World Youth Day 2013 theme song. After Mass, a spontaneous beach party erupted. The sun had risen to its blistering midday height, blanketing the beach in a growing heat wave. In response, thousands of overheated pilgrims jumped into the ocean to refresh themselves with cold water. Others stayed on the beach and danced as Catholic musicians performed for us from the sanctuary platform.

Although we were still hungry, we felt joy and peace from the spiritual nourishment we shared at Mass. We also felt physical relief from being able to move around more freely as the beach gradually emptied.

For more than an hour, our students waded in the water with fellow pilgrims from around the world, cooling off and splashing each other happily. Meanwhile, a Jesuit priest and I did a live beachside interview for EWTN's *Life on the Rock* television program, being rewarded with complimentary bottles of water. The water was the best part for me, as we had run out of liquids on the beach.

Copacabana felt like a fitting end to our long and grueling week. We had spent several days hauling ourselves around Rio, where the public transit system kept breaking down and running into delays. Rarely did we end up exactly where we wanted to be. Even our two attempts to visit the city's iconic statue of Christ the Redeemer had been thwarted, once by fog and once by an excessive number of pilgrims that stretched the wait into several hours beyond our departure time for the flight home.

Because the number of World Youth Day pilgrims overwhelmed the city, our group of fifty students and chaperones had also been bumped from the nice parish gym where we were supposed to sleep during our first six nights in the city. Instead we ended up bunking down on the dirty floors of a public elementary school in one of Rio's slums — a *favela* where nightly sirens and gunshots obliged us to keep the front doors locked. There were bars on the windows.

Throughout the week, I took photographs and wrote a daily blog for our students' parents on the school website, giving them updates of our adventures. Wi-Fi service was almost nonexistent.

We went to Copacabana Beach several times for evening liturgies, including a welcome Mass with the local archbishop and a live Stations of the Cross with Pope Francis. At the latter, a flatbed trailer carried the actors and actresses dramatizing the last hours of Christ's life to different points along the beach, working up to a finale on the sanctuary platform where Francis awaited it.

In some ways, our frequent trips to Copacabana for liturgies were a nice change of pace from the slum where we stayed. Each morning that week, we took ice-cold showers in a rusty bathroom at the school. We celebrated Mass in a dingy gathering area, squatting in chairs designed for little children.

Some of our students got sick from gorging on junk food and catching germs in the streets. Our first aid kit soon yielded up most of its antibiotics, digestive medications, and salves for insect bites.

Yet in spite of these challenges, nobody wanted to quit. Every day we toured a different part of the city, visiting World Youth Day events and sites wherever we found them. Spontaneous encounters with youth groups from other countries, even from other Jesuit high schools in various parts of the world, marked our wanderings.

We ate whatever food we could find, from whoever was selling it. We stopped to pray or rest at whatever Catholic parishes we stumbled across. Every parish in the city was open to us.

One morning, as we rode the train from our slum to the city center, we saw the pope's police escort parked at a *favela* he was visiting near ours. Since the city's poor couldn't come to Francis, he had gone to them. He also visited a Franciscan ministry to drug addicts.

Despite spotty news and Internet service, we later learned Francis had exhorted Catholics in a speech that day to "flip the tortilla," asking us to shake things up and make a joyful noise.

A real tortilla would have delighted our students, who spent most of the trip alternating between fatigue and hunger as we fought our way through endless crowds on the public transit system. For our students, it was an exciting life experience outside the comfortable routine of home. For the Jesuits and young adult chaperones, all veterans of high school trips, it was a new threshold of exhaustion.

We certainly felt like we were on the margins that week, whether we wanted to be there or not. Tired and hungry, we shared the life of the city and its pilgrims for seven days, but we also shared the life of the slums in a small way. Each morning brought fresh adventures and new encounters with the needy.

From Paraguay to the Slums of Rio

By heading into Rio's slums to visit the poor that week, it appeared to us that Francis was living out his message: Go to the margins and see whom you find there. Don't give advice or try to interpret the suffering of others, but place yourself with them in solidarity. Talk and pray with them.

After a weeklong pilgrimage to ruined Jesuit missionary sites in Paraguay, including the magnificent Iguazu Falls and other places depicted in the film *The Mission*, our little group already felt a bit on the margins by the time we arrived in Rio for World Youth Day.

During the week in Paraguay, daily prayer and faith sharing accompanied our interactions with people. We even prayed before the exposed heart of St. Roque González, a Jesuit missionary known as the "apostle of Paraguay," in its glass reliquary at a Jesuit high school in the capital of Asunción. In 1628, an Indian witch doctor, jealous of González's influence over the natives, conspired successfully to kill the priest with an axe.

In Paraguay, the unexpected became routine. At one point, our bus broke down, and we went on a five-mile hike through the subtropical fields and forests, meeting more farm animals than people along the way. Another day, we celebrated Mass in the grassy ruins of an ancient Jesuit mission church.

We met indigenous peoples. Coming to a Guarani Indian village, accessible only by foot paths and bridges through the forest some distance from the nearest active Jesuit mission in San Ingacio Guazu, we spent a day bartering with the chief as our boys kicked a soccer ball around with the village kids. The village consisted of a few dirt paths and thatched-roof huts; the chief wore a soccer jersey.

Our students loved the first week in Paraguay perhaps even more than the second week in Rio. Like Francis, they seemed to enjoy visiting with people more than attending the big public events.

And the parents supported our students. Rather than spending money on a summer vacation to Disney or Cancún, the families of our students paid to send them on a religious pilgrimage to visit Jesuit missions and pray with the Holy Father in South America.

Instead of playing video games and sitting on the couch all summer, our students spent two weeks living in a foreign-language environment, sleeping on trains, and singing songs with young people from other countries. They loved it.

But Pope Francis, then seventy-six years old, seemed to be outpacing all of us.

Using his police escort to full advantage, Francis traveled all over Rio during the week of World Youth Day, appearing to us in fleeting glimpses on news broadcasts and at the beach each night as we crowded to attend the various liturgies he led there.

Despite an exhausting schedule, the Holy Father took his time with each person he met. On the day his plane landed in Rio, admirers mobbed Francis's car when it took a wrong turn after leaving the airport, alarming security personnel. Smiling, Francis simply rolled down his window and started chatting with people who rushed up to the car. He was in no hurry.

Large crowds greeted him everywhere with a musical chant, delivered in a cadence familiar to World Youth Day veterans: "Papa Francisco!"

In the open motorcade that took Francis to the sanctuary platform at Copacabana Beach each day, he frequently stopped to bless babies and talk with onlookers.

One night, our group watched in surprise as pilgrims scrambled up trees along the beach to get a better look at Francis. Like Zacchaeus the tax collector, a short man who climbed a tree to see Jesus in Luke 19, they were rewarded by frequent stops from the papal motorcade as they waved from the branches.

We could feel the excitement in the air. When Francis stopped unexpectedly right in front of us that night, the screaming crowd around us surged forward with a groan, causing a screaming woman at the front to pass out from excitement. Paramedics loaded her onto a nearby ambulance.

The pope gave several public talks every bit as electrifying as his personal interactions, delivering the exhortations in a form of Spanish so clear that almost anyone could understand him just by listening to the tone of his words and watching his body language.

Go to the margins, Francis kept saying in Spanish, repeating it in his talks and in the closing Mass homily. See
whom you find and hear what they have to say. Share the joy
of your faith, using words if necessary.

Who was on the margins in Rio? What did they have to say
to our group? And what could we possibly offer them in return?

Even as our South American pilgrimage was ending, our
journey to God was only beginning.

Waking Up to Poverty

But back to Copacabana Beach, where we slept before the papal Mass. When I awoke on the beach that morning, shivering
in my black Jesuit cassock and poncho in the winds of Brazil's summery winter, something felt wrong. The sky above my
head was still dark. I wasn't supposed to be up yet.

Forcing myself into a sitting position, I suddenly realized the freezing tide of the ocean had washed over half of our
group. Another Jesuit was shouting for everyone to wake up
and move.

It turned out that our group — like hundreds of others
along the shoreline — was sleeping too close to the water's
edge for high tide.

That tide washed away some personal items and all of
our boxes of food, but it failed to sweep away any freshmen,
despite jokes to that effect from a few upperclassmen. It was
sometime after 3:00 a.m., and most of our fellow pilgrims
remained fast asleep.

After taking stock of our losses, we moved to the road-
side sidewalk at the edge of the beach to dry out and close
our eyes for the last few hours of darkness before Pope Francis
came for Mass.

Clark Bulleit, a football player who eventually became
valedictorian of his class, later described this day as the happi-

est moment of his life. In his valedictory address at graduation in May 2015, Bulleit said:

> So what does make me happy? Long walks on the beach and beautiful sunsets? No. Actually, the time in my life where I was most happy, I was sleeping on the sidewalk, dehydrated and malnourished during my trip to Brazil for World Youth Day. I was happy because, there, I was completely unconcerned with myself, and in full communion with my fellow people and God himself.

Pushed to the edge of his personal limits, Bulleit had somehow realized his longing for God in this moment, and he woke up on the sidewalk in a deep state of consolation.

Not all of us slumbered so peacefully. Despite all of my Jesuit mind tricks, I couldn't go back to sleep again after we moved from the beach.

Huddled on the sidewalk, I surrendered myself instead to the various thoughts drifting through my mind. Trying to forget the pin pricks in my back caused by sleeping on the sand, I began meditating on the events of our trip.

At sunrise a few hours later, I suddenly recalled the question my student had asked me in March. "What if the next pope is a Jesuit?"

Yeah, right, I remembered thinking. What if pigs could fly? God sure does have a sense of humor.

The thought occurred to me that, had I seen Pope Francis riding the Buenos Aires subway during his time as archbishop, I might not have paid any attention to him. But now he was the Vicar of Christ, the successor of St. Peter, preparing to celebrate Mass with three million of us on a cold and windy beach that would soon be bathed in a warm sunlight.

Had I seen Jesus Christ on the subway in Rio that week, I'd like to think I might have recognized him. But I'm not so sure. As St. John the Evangelist knew, it's hard to see the invisible God until we recognize him in our visible neighbors.

Even St. Thomas the Apostle struggled to recognize the risen Christ in the witness of his brothers and sisters.

As I thought about these things on the sidewalk, it occurred to me that common desires had kept our group together in Rio: our shared longings for food, shelter, medicine, transportation, and dry clothing. Like the residents of the slum Francis visited, we lived in constant need, isolated within a country that didn't really see or understand us. While we didn't suffer as deeply as the city's poor, we felt closer to God's people in our experiences of deprivation of things we normally took for granted — things such as hot showers, drinkable water, climate control, and readily available food. But it also struck me that there were deeper longings, hidden beneath the surface, uniting our hearts and minds on pilgrimage: God's longing for us, our longing for God, and our longing to bring God's love to others.

Although we had traveled to South America to see Pope Francis, we gradually realized it was Jesus Christ himself who awaited us there. On this journey to God, we immersed ourselves wholeheartedly in the experience, stirring the deepest desires of our hearts. And we started to see how God was responding.

As Pope Francis emphasizes, to long for God makes us long to share God's love with others. This longing conjures up deep emotions in all of us, particularly surrounding our experiences of sin and grace.

Sin, the Obstacle That Distorts Our Longing

For Francis, who often talks about the reality of the devil, sin and grace are more than ideas in a book. In his view, deeply rooted in his Catholic and Jesuit traditions, sin and grace manifest themselves within us as attitudes of selfishness and love. While sin diverts our longings to self-centered goals, grace fuels the longing for God that empowers us to go to the margins as missionaries.

How do Catholics understand sin? Some of us look to definitions. The *Catechism of the Catholic Church* defines sin as the "failure in genuine love for God and neighbor caused by a perverse attachment to certain goods" (CCC 1849). Sin "turns our hearts away" from God's love (CCC 1850).

Building on these meanings, Pope Francis describes sin as the selfish act of hurting others on purpose. Sinful attachment turns us inward rather than outward, causing us to ignore people in need. He writes:

> To go out of ourselves and to join others is healthy for us. To be self-enclosed is to taste the bitter poison of immanence, and humanity will be worse for every selfish choice we make. (*Evangelii Gaudium* 87)

Francis calls sin a "selfish choice" rooted in our short-sighted longings for false idols like money, sex, and power. Indeed, he has consistently rejected the false idols of secular materialism, noting that too many of us spend more time obsessing over our pets and cosmetics than caring for our fellow human beings. He adds: "The thirst for power and possessions knows no limits" (*Evangelii Gaudium* 57).

Here the pope evokes a key theme from his Ignatian spiritual tradition: the satanic temptations of riches, honors, and pride.

For the Jesuit founder, St. Ignatius of Loyola, the selfishness of sin is inextricably bound up with these three temptations to indulge our feelings of entitlement over others. Such feelings originate not in a healthy self-esteem, but in the assumption that we deserve more from life than we have received and more than others possess.

St. Ignatius notes, as does Pope Francis, that nothing is ever good enough for the selfish person, whose noble longings gradually become reoriented (disordered) toward secondary goods at the cost of our primary relationships. In a letter to a Portuguese Jesuit dated March 18, 1542, Ignatius declares that "the most abominable of sins" is ingratitude, or the habitual refusal to acknowledge the gifts God has given us.

Like the unfulfilled corporate executive, unloved by his parents and family, who always needs to buy "just one more" house or car. Or the eighteen-year-old American athlete who squanders a multimillion dollar professional sports contract after being drafted out of high school. They earned their money, the world tells us, so why can't they enjoy it?

Ingratitude thrives whenever we give free reign to our self-centered longings. It feeds our disordered craving for possessions rather than loving relationships, affirming our selfish longing for instant gratification at the expense of God and others.

If our longing for God leads us to the margins in places like Rio de Janeiro, then our longing for possessions often fuels a lasting ingratitude that closes our hearts to others. Francis argues in his encyclical *Laudato Si'* (May 24, 2015) that this longing, writ large, drives the consumerism that destroys our planet's natural resources and exploits the poor. But he also says we can break this cycle if we turn back to God.

From Sin to Grace

As he showed us in Rio, Pope Francis knows how fearful narcissism dominates our hearts in a consumer society, steering our longings away from Gospel joy. But he also recognizes that we can accept our selfishness as a positive challenge, using our own painful experiences of sin's effects as a motivation to reject its hold over us. Rather than a burden, sin can be a challenge to redirect our longings to God, reopening our hearts to his grace.

The first step from sin to grace, as Francis reminded us in Brazil, is admitting to ourselves we are sinners in need of God's mercy. Once we unmask the selfishness we ignore in ourselves and condemn in others, Francis suggests we can then use our experience of sin as a useful kick in the pants.

Francis himself demonstrated this healthy self-awareness one year during Lent, going to confession publicly in St. Peter's Basilica.

While leading a penance service there on March 28, 2014, the pope, along with sixty-one other priests, had moved toward confessional boxes and chairs near the walls to offer the sacrament for individual penitents. But as the papal master of ceremonies showed the Holy Father to the place he would use to hear confessions, Francis pointed to another confessional nearby, insisting that he himself would be the first to confess.

As Francis knelt in front of the wooden confessional box, his white-clad back to the congregation, photographers and videographers captured the unusual moment. Although Francis goes to confession every two weeks, even the most recent popes have rarely been seen confessing their sins to a fellow priest in public.

For his part, the priest to whom Francis confessed was a little nonplused by having the pope as a penitent. When the encounter was finished, he grasped the pope's hands and kissed them in reverence.

By living only for ourselves, many of us allow our sins to become habitual and thoughtless vices, abandoning humble self-awareness as we concentrate our longings on enhancing our own sense of wealth and prestige. But the example of Francis says we can begin to overcome these selfish longings if we learn how to expose them to the world — and to ourselves — for what they really are.

St. Ignatius notes in the "Two Standards" meditation — these standards are the battle flag of Christ and the battle flag of Satan, between which all of us must choose — that after we gain riches and honors, the Evil One tempts us more easily to pride, the sin of thinking we are better than others because we have acquired more stuff and respect than they have. Rather than love people on society's margins as Christ does — including not only the materially poor, but also, for example, the lonely or bullied or socially awkward — we learn to despise them as much as we implicitly despise ourselves. True empathy thus becomes impossible, at least until we rekindle our longing for God.

From Pride to Humility

In little ways, all of us practice the sin of pride in our lives, as when we pay more attention to our gadgets and possessions than to our relationships. Or when Catholic teachers "play the professor," as Pope Francis put it on a visit to Ecuador in July 2015, talking down to young people to feel superior to them rather than striving to reach their hearts with Christ's transformative love.

For Pope Francis as for St. Ignatius, our downward spiral into pride begins with our desires for money and fame rather than for loving relationships — a disordered longing for idols that is always demonic, but often grabs our hearts because we do not recognize it as evil.

While horror movies like *The Exorcist* depict Jesuits as demon fighters, the devil is more than a Hollywood villain or theological concept for Pope Francis. The devil's chief activity in today's global society, as Francis preached it to us at World Youth Day 2013, is to cultivate a self-despairing consumerism among Christians that redirects our hearts away from God and those who need his love.

In the pope's eyes, only a humble awareness of our fundamental human equality as sinners in need of God's mercy can reverse this sinful movement of our longings away from God. Once we are hardened in the selfish and ungrateful conviction that we are entitled to more than others, we risk shutting our hearts to God's love for good, destroying ourselves and our planet in the process.

Rather than being struck by lightning in divine punishment for our sins, Francis notes that we find ourselves miserable and our relationships in chaos when we act selfishly, robbing us of Gospel joy. Our lives become empty and meaningless because we love nothing and no one other than ourselves. It is precisely in this experience of misery that God challenges us to turn our hearts back to his grace.

The Grace of Love

For Pope Francis, love is the opposite of selfishness, being rooted in our longing for God and in our experiences of his grace. Grace calls us out of sin, builds upon our longing for God, and finally bears fruit in the love we show our neighbors on the margins.

So what, then, is grace?

The *Catechism* defines grace as "*favor, the free and undeserved help* that God gives us" (CCC 1996, emphasis in original) to move from selfishness to selflessness in our lifelong path to holiness. If sin directs our longings away from the God of the margins, inviting us to seek fulfillment only in ourselves, then grace moves us outward to love those who we recognize are as incomplete as we are.

Grace is rooted in the self-giving love of Christ's sacrifice on the cross. God's longing for us on the cross, answered by the grace of our longing for him, is the enemy of selfishness. We can cooperate with this grace by embracing Christ's cross in our own lives, giving ourselves to others just as he gives himself to us in self-sacrifice.

Like the high school senior who helps out an awkward freshman rather than bully him for the amusement of others. Or the mom who takes her eighth-grade son to one more football game, even though she hasn't had an afternoon to herself in ten years.

We all have the ability to cooperate with God's grace, provided we make space for it in our hearts. Grace doesn't ask if a person is worthy of love, but assumes it. Selfless love is not finally motivated by our fear of hell or desire for heaven, as helpful as those things are for spiritual beginners, but by our longing for the good of others — especially the needy — that is rooted in our deeper longing for God.

The Love of God

Our human longing to give and receive God's love recalls a poem by the great Gerard Manley Hopkins, S.J., called *O Deus Ego Amo Te*.

O God, I love thee, I love thee —
Not out of hope of heaven for me
Nor fearing not to love and be
In the everlasting burning.

Thou, thou, my Jesus, after me
Didst reach thine arms out dying,
For my sake sufferedst nails and lance,
Mocked and marred countenance,
Sorrows passing number,
Sweat, and care and cumber,
Yea, and death, and this for me.
And thou couldst see me sinning:

Then I, why should I not love thee,
Jesu, so much in love with me?

Not for heaven's sake; not to be
Out of hell by loving thee;
Not for any gains I see;
But just the way that thou didst me
I do love and will love thee:

What must I love thee, Lord, for then?
For being my King and God. Amen.

For Hopkins, an English convert and Jesuit priest whose poetry outlived his unremarkable teaching career, to love God *simply for being God* constitutes the highest expression of our human longing for the divine. God's love is never conditioned on our success or failure in his service, and so we needn't "perform" for him through the adoption of a forced attitude of compliant servitude toward others. Only by loving others for their own sake, as Christ loves us, can we fulfill our longing for God.

As we strive to love people on the margins in this profound way, Pope Francis warns Catholics in a famously dense passage to avoid any form of pharisaical worldliness that makes us feel superior to others because we know more or follow the rules of our faith more closely than them. He writes:

> This worldliness can be fueled in two deeply interrelated ways. One is the attraction of gnosticism, a purely subjective faith whose only interest is a certain experience or a set of ideas and bits of information which are meant to console and enlighten, but which ultimately keep one imprisoned in his or her own thoughts and feelings.
>
> The other is the self-absorbed promethean neopelagianism of those who ultimately trust only in their own powers and feel superior to others because they observe certain rules or remain intransigently faithful to a particular Catholic style from the past.

> A supposed soundness of doctrine or discipline leads instead to a narcissistic and authoritarian elitism, whereby instead of evangelizing, one analyzes and classifies others, and instead of opening the door to grace, one exhausts his or her energies in inspecting and verifying. (*Evangelii Gaudium* 94)

Here we see that the desire to analyze others rather than help them is another sinful temptation blocking true evangelization. Christ's self-giving love never keeps people at a distance through sectarian and intellectual defenses, but engages them in relationship. To love in this interpersonal way is above all else a grace — a gift from God that we must accept and cultivate, but that we cannot force.

Like Hopkins, Francis invites Catholics to lead self-giving lives, appreciating Christ's deep personal love for us and acting freely on our longing to love him in return. With confidence, the pope insists our longing for God can build on human nature as a grace that leads us passionately to the margins, where we find people who are like ourselves in every way that matters. When we long for God, we soon long to share God's love with others, giving without counting the cost.

God's Desires

As my students and I learned on Copacabana Beach, the longing for God is present in every person, even if one is unaware of it. And we Catholics are called not only to love those on the margins who follow our faith, but also those who feel wounded by religion and distant from God. They are God's children too.

To recall an expression popular in Catholic social justice circles, "We love others because *we* are Catholic, not because *they* are Catholic." As missionaries, we accept Christ's invitation to the margins not merely because we expect a reward for going or fear a punishment for not going. Nor do we go out of a false sense of obligation that breeds resentment. We go because we love God more than life itself and because we long to share his love for us with others.

For human beings alive to God's desires for us, our longing for the divine brings our relationship with Christ beyond doctrine and duty to experience. As Francis notes in *The Joy of the Gospel,* authentic evangelization flows from our religious experiences of Christ's self-giving love in our lives. He writes:

> We have a treasure of life and love which cannot deceive, and a message which cannot mislead or disappoint. It penetrates to the depths of our hearts, sustaining and ennobling us. It is a truth which is never out of date because it reaches that part of us which nothing else can reach. Our infinite sadness can only be cured by an infinite love. (*Evangelii Gaudium* 265)

Christ's deep longing to be with the needy continues to resonate in our consumerist world. If we unplug from our material possessions and plug our hearts into the people around us, Francis suggests we might glimpse Jesus in the face of the marginalized whose suffering was previously invisible to us. Gratefully recognizing Jesus in our brothers and sisters, we can find fulfillment in our joyful experiences of sharing with others the good news of God's desire for our happiness.

In the meantime, Francis invites Catholics to pray for the grace to long for relationships more than for vanities, rejecting superficial worldliness in favor of loving action. He writes:

> God save us from a worldly Church with superficial spiritual and pastoral trappings! This stifling worldliness can only be healed by breathing in the pure air of the Holy Spirit who frees us from self-centeredness cloaked in an outward religiosity bereft of God. Let

us not allow ourselves to be robbed of the Gospel!
(*Evangelii Gaudium* 97)

One final story may illustrate what it looks like to share
our longing for God in today's culture. Not long after World
Youth Day 2013, Pope Francis was riding through the Italian
countryside when his motorcade approached a small cluster
of well-wishers. Waving signs that asked Francis to bless a sick
family member, this group of rural Italians clearly wanted this
young woman to feel closer to God's love by meeting the pope.

Many celebrities, politicians, and billionaires would have
kept driving. Not Francis.

To the Italians' surprise and delight, the pope stopped
his car, rolled down the backseat window, and spoke to the
woman. He blessed her warmly as the family wept in happiness. A video of the encounter, taken on a camera phone,
quickly found its way to the Internet.

Such throwaway moments remind us that Jesus spent
most of his life in a backwater village, never traveling more
than a few dozen miles from home. He wasn't rich or powerful
in his lifetime, nor was he honored, but he was a man of deep
desires for human happiness. He shared God's love with his
followers and inspired them to share it with others.

Jesus probably even slept on the sand once or twice, cold
and hungry, to be with his people.

We can do the same today. If we stay focused on our
desire for God and, more deeply, on God's desires for us,
we may find ourselves capable of greater things than we ever
imagined — even if we are only able to share Christ's love in
small ways. We can begin to fulfill our longing for God right
here and now, without needing to attend World Youth Day
in faraway places like Brazil or Poland.

For as the Bible says, "Blessed are you who are now hungry, for you will be satisfied" (Lk 2:21).

CHAPTER TWO

CLOSENESS

---

*To be evangelizers of souls, we need to develop a spiritual
taste for being close to people's lives and to discover that
this is itself a source of greater joy. Mission is at once a
passion for Jesus and a passion for his people.*

*When we stand before Jesus crucified, we see the
depth of his love which exalts and sustains us, but at the
same time, unless we are blind, we begin to realize that
Jesus' gaze, burning with love, expands to embrace all
his people. We realize once more that he wants to make
use of us to draw closer to his beloved people. He takes us
from the midst of his people and he sends us to his people;
without this sense of belonging we cannot understand our
deepest identity.* (Evangelii Gaudium *268*)

During the annual Easter Triduum, Pope Francis participates
in a custom he started during the first year of his papacy, visiting a Roman prison to celebrate Holy Thursday Mass.

The visit is rich in symbolism, both old and new.

On the Roman Catholic liturgical calendar, Holy Thursday occurs a few days before Easter Sunday and commemorates the Last Supper of Jesus Christ with his apostles.

This Evening Mass of the Lord's Supper reaches its high
point in an ancient ceremony where the celebrating priest
washes the feet of twelve people from the congregation, symbolizing Jesus washing the feet of his twelve apostles in St.
John's Gospel. Jesus concluded this ritual by giving his apostles
the *mandatum* or new commandment to "love one another …
as I have loved you" (Jn 13:34).

Holy Thursday concludes Lent and Holy Week — the most sacred time of year for Christians — by recalling the last peaceful hours of apostolic fellowship before Christ's passion. It also begins the Easter Triduum, a three-day celebration of Christ's passion, death, and resurrection that culminates in Easter Sunday.

Video footage of Francis washing the feet of inmates in Rebibbia prison has appeared in newscasts on Holy Thursday each year, giving us images of Gospel witness more eloquent and powerful than words.

In the April 2015 video, we see the humbled — and humble — Francis kneel to wash the feet of twelve prisoners and a baby, going slowly from inmate to inmate with a basin of water. We see him wash the feet of women as well as men, Muslims as well as Catholics, and greet each one with a smile.

As we watch Francis wash the feet of one female prisoner with her baby, the woman quietly wipes away streams of tears, profoundly moved by the experience. Here is the spiritual head of the world's 1.2 billion Catholics, God's representative on earth, physically closer to her than any other world leader will likely ever be. And by washing her feet, Francis is doing what Jesus commanded: coming close to God's people in an act of love and service.

Later that same weekend, in his brief remarks at the Easter Vigil Mass on Saturday night, Francis said the following about entering into the mystery of God's love:

> To enter into the mystery, we need humility, the lowliness to abase ourselves, to come down from the pedestal of our "I" which is so proud, of our presumption; the humility not to take ourselves so seriously, recognizing who we really are: creatures with strengths and weaknesses, sinners in need of forgiveness. (Homily for the Easter Vigil, April 4, 2015)

So God's love summons us to embrace not just a theory of joy and longing, but an active love that appears in experiences of warm physical closeness to God's people. "Only on the basis of this real and sincere closeness can we properly accompany the poor on their path of liberation," the pope writes in his exhortation (*Evangelii Gaudium* 199).

For the Christian who receives and shares God's love, nothing replaces the personal experience of God "coming down from the pedestal" to meet us where we are. And for Francis, the best way to develop a taste for being close to others in their brokenness is to spend time with them on the margins.

Learning from Closeness

As pope, Francis has consistently demonstrated what he means by closeness to God's people.

In one iconic moment early in his papacy, television cameras and photographers recorded Francis embracing a severely disabled boy after the pope celebrated his first Easter Sunday Mass in St. Peter's Square. The image traveled swiftly around the world.

Paul Gondreau, a theology professor at Providence College in Rhode Island, lifted his son Dominic toward Pope Francis for this embrace and a kiss. Dominic, aged eight at the time, was born prematurely and has cerebral palsy.

Professor Gondreau later told the media that he and his wife, Christiana, were not expecting this encounter when they came to St. Peter's with their five children for Easter Mass. Because security protocols required the family to separate, Professor Gondreau had taken his son to an area designated for adults and children with disabilities. That's where they caught the pope's eye as he passed.

In countless encounters like this one, Francis has never hesitated to reach out to the disabled, abandoned, or disfigured people our society has marginalized.

When I was a young Jesuit novice in my first year of seminary life, I had a similar experience of closeness during one memorable assignment at a Christian community for people with intellectual disabilities.

Arriving at L'Arche Mobile in March 2006, I had just come off my first series of boot camp experiences (called "probations" or "experiments" in Jesuit lingo) designed to initiate me in religious life, but I was still feeling unsettled in my vocation.

While I had the desire to be a priest, my Jesuit life in those early days remained a set of beautiful ideals about vowed life that existed mostly in my head, undisturbed by any significant life experiences. I had only been a Jesuit for seven months and had no idea what to expect in my new assignment.

At L'Arche, I soon found that working with adults with Down Syndrome and similar challenges was different than working with other adults and children. Closeness was more challenging because the emotional and physical demands were so great.

More than anything else, the deep loneliness of feeling abandoned by their families affected the lives of the middle-aged residents, who lived in four houses with their caregivers and were nearing the end of their predicted life spans. Although many of their parents had died or become too old to care for them anymore, the residents generally didn't understand why their families weren't there.

It was an aging community. Many of the L'Arche Mobile residents or "core members" were in wheelchairs, needing to be lifted and carried to various places. They required constant attention, in a very close way, for the simple things most of us take for granted.

For six weeks I lived in a little white house with four core members, sharing a routine of fellowship and prayer with them. After the required training sessions, I started driving them around in a van with a hydraulic wheelchair lift and working with them at the community activity center. Stripped of my comfortable seminary routine of prayers and books, I applied myself to household tasks and projects, fixing what needed fixing and painting what needed painting. I cooked meals and drove people to and from various places, including church and restaurants where outsiders stared at us. I helped residents take baths, brush their teeth, and use the toilet.

But as time went on, I learned that my real contribution came in spending time with the people of L'Arche, not in fixing their material problems. These men and women, for their part, were entirely comfortable being themselves. They helped me appreciate my own brokenness and need for love.

If I evangelized anyone at L'Arche, it was because I grew close to them through sharing our common human struggles with one another — not through any of my worldly accomplishments. My education, training, and other achievements meant nothing there.

Jean Vanier, the Catholic philosopher who founded L'Arche in the 1960s when he invited two intellectually disabled men to live with him at a house in France, wrote several books about the paradoxical truth that sharing our weakness and struggles unites us more than sharing our strengths and successes. By the time I finished at L'Arche, I understood better what Vanier meant.

As I got to know each individual in the community, I grew in a love for each one that was close and personal. Their joys and struggles, their very direct and immediate needs remained a constant challenge, pushing me to go outside of myself. Some of the messes I cleaned up, both spiritual and physical, remain impossible to describe.

At one point, as I was giving a bath to a middle-aged man and then helping him get dressed and back into his wheelchair, I had a powerful sense of gratitude for the trust he gave me. Rather than complaining about things as he often did, he stayed silent as I helped him, apparently recognizing my good intentions toward him. While I had thought I was being patient with him, I now realizeed he was being patient with me as well.

When I returned to the novitiate a month later, it felt like I was a changed man, happier and closer to God than I was before the trip. I had forgotten myself at L'Arche, but in a good way, as I had learned how to get closer to God and his people in ministry. The trip stayed with me in prayer too.

On our annual eight-day retreat later that spring, I experienced a powerful meditation in which I saw Jesus Christ in the face of a disabled man I had assisted. The image suddenly jumped into my memory while I was praying the Stations of the Cross in our Jesuit cemetery. Meditating over Christ's first fall on the way of the cross, I experienced the grace of suffering with others as the memory of this man came to my imagination, and I felt a deeper appreciation for the love shared by many families with Down Syndrome members.

When Pope Francis talks about closeness to people on the margins, it's partly because of L'Arche that I can appreciate a little bit of what he means. The pope, a former Jesuit novice master and provincial who sent many seminarians to places like L'Arche, could be talking about his own Jesuit formation as well as my own when he writes:

Being a disciple means being constantly ready to bring the love of Jesus to others, and this can happen unexpectedly and in any place: on the street, in a city square, during work, on a journey. (*Evangelii Gaudium* 127)

The Jesuit Pope

As a Jesuit novice, my experiences of closeness to God's people also included weekly visits to homebound parishioners in rural Grand Coteau, Louisiana, the site of our novitiate and where I, along with the other novices, made the thirty-day silent retreat (the *Spiritual Exercises of St. Ignatius*) that every Jesuit completes twice in his life.

Grand Coteau, a sleepy Cajun hamlet with one thousand people and one religion, Catholicism, felt to many of us like the land that time forgot. Our home at St. Charles College had been founded in the 1880s as a Jesuit boarding school for boys before being converted into a novitiate in 1920. It was also home to a Jesuit parish, St. Charles Borromeo, and to Our Lady of the Oaks Jesuit retreat house.

Graves dating back to the Civil War — including that of Fr. Tom Sherman, S.J., son of General William Tecumseh Sherman — lined our walking paths. Tolling bells, dusty books, and old wooden desks marked our daily routine. Retreatants often wandered the grounds, lost in prayer.

In the first months of novitiate, we studied the constitutions and vows of our Jesuit order, engaged in faith sharing, and hosted a Christmas party for elderly parishioners. We ate exotic foods like alligator, made pastoral visits to nursing homes, and eventually ministered together in the Rio Grande Valley of Texas for an intensive probation among the poor.

For two months in Texas we worked in hospitals, parish catechetical ministry, a juvenile prison, and a hospice for the dying.

Pope Francis underwent the same basic program of long intellectual formation, tempered by immersion with the poor, that every other Jesuit in the world experiences. He made the thirty-day retreat, took simple perpetual vows after a two-year novitiate, studied philosophy, and taught high school chemistry as "Mr. Bergoglio" before proceeding to theology studies and ordination.

Unlike most Jesuits, however, Francis acquired some unusually big responsibilities as a young priest in the heady decade after Vatican II, assuming leadership of the Society of Jesus in a nation at war with itself.

Only four years after being ordained a priest, Francis found himself appointed provincial superior of the Argentine Jesuits at the unusually tender age of thirty-six. Serving as provincial for the customary six-year term from 1973 to 1979, Fr. Bergoglio spent much of his time protecting priests and others who were working for the poor from government death squads during Argentina's so-called "dirty war."

The experience of Gonzalo Mosca, a member of a leftist military group, was typical of those Bergoglio rescued. At the risk of his own life, Fr. Bergoglio accompanied Mosca twenty miles to the seminary outside of Buenos Aires, instructing him on what to do if soldiers stopped the car: "Tell them you're going on a spiritual retreat." Mosca, then twenty-seven years old, hid at the seminary until the priest was able to get him a plane ticket out of the country.

During the 1980s, things calmed down for the young Fr. Bergoglio, but he continued to assume positions of responsibility in the Society of Jesus. From 1980 to 1986, he worked in Jesuit formation again as rector of a major seminary and later served as a spiritual director for all sorts of people, who found themselves drawn to the approachable "Fr. Jorge."

Recognizing his gifts for connecting with people on a personal level, Pope John Paul II eventually appointed Fr. Bergoglio a bishop in 1992 and a cardinal in 2001. As archbishop of Buenos Aires, Cardinal Bergoglio later made a point of being available to all of the priests in his care, giving them his cell phone number and encouraging them to call at any hour of the day.

In his time as a priest and even as a bishop, Francis made countless friends who were street people, including a homeless woman in Buenos Aires whom he visited daily outside of the cathedral and who missed him greatly after he was elected pope.

He has kept up these habits since his election, often dropping in on homeless shelters and social service agencies during his travels and, demonstrating another aspect of closeness, even staying in touch with his fellow Jesuits. Besides popping into Jesuit Refugee Services in Rome for visits, he has made surprise trips to Jesuit headquarters to celebrate the feast day of St. Ignatius and to spend time with his religious brothers, sometimes giving the bemused Jesuit general only a few minutes' notice. He seems to value the mutual support of his Jesuit friendships.

Called by Mercy

On a more somber note, Francis has also stayed close to victims of violence and poverty, calling particular attention to the growing refugee crisis worldwide.

He has forcefully condemned Italian mafia violence against the poor and spoken out for the rights of refugees — including the thousands of shipwrecked North Africans whose deaths he commemorated in a Mass on the island of Lampedusa in July 2013.

"To the criminals and all their accomplices, I, today, humbly and as a brother, repeat: convert yourselves to love and justice," Pope Francis told the mafia in a speech in Naples. "It is possible to return to honesty. The tears of the mothers of Naples are asking this of you."

In the Mass at Lampedusa, Francis prayed: "Lord, in this liturgy, a penitential liturgy, we beg forgiveness for our indifference to so many of our brothers and sisters."

As pope, the model for Francis's outreach to God's people remains Jesus Christ himself:

> Jesus himself is the model of this method of evangelization which brings us to the very heart of his people. How good it is for us to contemplate the closeness which he shows to everyone!...
>
> Moved by his example, we want to enter fully into the fabric of society, sharing the lives of all, listening to their concerns, helping them materially and spiritually in their needs, rejoicing with those who rejoice, weeping with those who weep; arm in arm with others, we are committed to building a new world. (*Evangelii Gaudium* 269)

The pope's own experiences of suffering and poverty undoubtedly influenced his sensitivity to the needs of the marginalized. The son of poor Italian immigrants who lived off a railroad worker's salary, he grew up during the regimes of Juan and Eva Peron and their successors — a setting very different from the enchanted fantasy of the musical "Evita." Ambitious military leaders were engaged in a desperate and ongoing power struggle as they exploited the dispossessed and crushed dissent.

Despite the hardships of his native land, Francis loved his country and people, and he flourished, perhaps in part because his Grandmother Rosa's strong Catholicism gave him stability.

It was an early experience of God's closeness that inspired his entry into the priesthood as well as the motto on his papal coat of arms — "*miserando atque eligendo*," which in Latin roughly means "by having mercy and by choosing him." The motto comes from a homily by St. Bede the Venerable on the call of St. Matthew: "Jesus saw the tax collector and by having mercy chose him as an Apostle, saying to him: Follow me."

Going to confession one day in 1953, the young future Pope Francis felt Jesus calling him personally in this way. He was sixteen years old that September 21, and on his way to join friends for Student's Day, an annual Argentine celebration marking the first day of spring in the Southern hemisphere. As he passed his parish church, he decided to drop in for confession.

Inside the church, Jorge Bergoglio discovered a priest he didn't know — the aging and ill Fr. Duarte, whom he recalls as an infectiously joyful person — and asked this cleric to hear his confession.

As he spoke with Fr. Duarte, Jorge experienced a profound longing to offer his life to the Church, and he decided to not go out with his friends that day. In his 2010 book-length interview with Sergio Rubin, then-Cardinal Bergoglio reflected on the experience. "In that Confession, something very rare happened to me," Bergloglio told Rubin. "It was a surprise, the astonishment of an encounter. I realized that God was waiting for me."

After receiving absolution for his sins, Jorge Bergoglio emerged from the sacrament with a sense of closeness to God's love and mercy as evoked by the words of Bede's homily. Feeling like St. Matthew, the tax collector whom Jesus called in mercy from his customs post (see Mt 9:9), he experienced an intimate sense of what he later described as God's "mercy-ing."

Further inspired by Caravaggio's painting *The Calling of St. Matthew* (1599–1600), the young Jorge felt sure Christ was speaking to him in this confession. Acting on his unexpected desire to "mercy" others as Christ had "mercied" him, he resolved to enter the seminary.

It is this personal experience of Jesus Christ's mercy that gives deeper meaning to Francis's words when he asks us as pope to practice solidarity. He writes:

Clearly Jesus does not want us to be grandees who look down upon others, but men and women of the people. This is not an idea of the Pope, or one pastoral option among others; they are injunctions contained in the word of God which are so clear, direct and convincing that they need no interpretations which might diminish their power to challenge us. Let us live them *sine glossa*, without commentaries. By so doing we will know the missionary joy of sharing life with God's faithful people as we strive to light a fire in the heart of the world. (*Evangelii Gaudium* 271)

For Francis, the quality of our missionary closeness to God's people depends on our own sense of God's closeness, and on our sense of God's love for us as forgiven sinners. When he speaks of following Christ's call to share our lives with the marginalized, Francis speaks from experience.

On this topic as on others, Francis speaks more pastorally than theologically or philosophically, often surprising Catholics with his frankness about himself and others. In one of his many off-the-cuff interviews, he once quipped in response to a question about a person who was gay and striving to live a celibate life: "Who am I to judge?"

Such a question invites us to ask ourselves other questions. Are we following God in freedom or simply appeasing him? If we are working sincerely in our lives to be closer to God and to his people, what more can God ask of us?

A Closeness That Evangelizes

Answering these sorts of questions on his own behalf, Pope Francis first seeks a personal closeness to the example of his recent predecessors, keenly aware that he did not invent evangelization.

While Francis has given the papacy a distinctive style and emphasis in calling Catholics to the margins, he has also walked a trail blazed by Pope St. John Paul II and Pope Benedict XVI. In particular, *Evangelii Gaudium* honors the work of these men by using their phrase "New Evangelization" to describe Francis's blueprint for missionary closeness in a field-hospital church. Far from *replacing* the New Evangelization, Francis preaches his vision of closeness to marginalized people as an *application* of it.

In the mind of Francis, ever conscious of his role as successor of St. Peter, his own closeness to God's people requires that he be close to the teachings of his immediate papal predecessors and to the vision of the Second Vatican Council. By calling on *all* baptized Christians to be missionary disciples who are close to the needy, he invites us to revisit the New Evangelization and Vatican II's universal call to holiness in light of our own experiences of Jesus. Francis writes:

> The new evangelization calls for personal involvement on the part of each of the baptized. Every Christian is challenged, here and now, to be actively engaged in evangelization; indeed, anyone who has truly experienced God's saving love does not need much time or lengthy training to go out and proclaim that love. (*Evangelii Gaudium* 120)

If Pope St. John Paul II was the diocesan bishop who strengthened the institutional Church against Communism, and Benedict XVI was the theology professor who gave us beautiful insights, then Francis is the Jesuit novice master sending all of us on mission — to places like L'Arche and poor enclaves and countries everywhere, but also to our own families and neighborhoods. He has put his own spin on the New Evangelization.

In whatever situations we find ourselves, Francis invites us to hear Christ's voice and follow it to the margins, being close not only to other believers, but also to all people as members of the same human family who live and work together. He writes:

> All of us are called to offer others an explicit witness to the saving love of the Lord, who despite our imperfections offers us his closeness, his word and his strength, and gives meaning to our lives. In your heart you know that it is not the same to live without him; what you have come to realize, what has helped you to live and given you hope, is what you also need to communicate to others. (*Evangelii Gaudium* 121)

If Francis wants all people of good will to embrace this solidarity, it doesn't mean he endorses all political or religious beliefs (for example, he has opposed same-sex marriage politically in Argentina and elsewhere while at the same time reaching out to gay people). But it does mean Francis loves everyone, wants to be close to them, and wants us to find opportunities to grow closer to others as well.

In November 2014, when Francis told the Ecumenical Patriarch Bartholomew that there are "no conditions" for reunion between the Catholic and Orthodox Churches, he illustrated this attitude by bowing his head to the patriarch and requesting a blessing "for me and the Church of Rome." The split between Western and Eastern Christianity, ongoing since 1054, remains of special concern to Francis. Particularly close to Byzantine Rite Catholics during his time as archbishop of Buenos Aires, he lifted a Vatican ban on ordination of married Eastern Catholic clergy outside of their traditional territories shortly before his visit to Bartholomew in Istanbul.

Being united to God's people with this kind of humility means we will sometimes get our hands dirty. We will walk with the suffering and open our hearts to them, even at the risk of being theologically imprecise. We will heal on the Sabbath and eat without washing. We will meet people we do not like or normally spend time around.

But at the end of our lives, as Bl. Mother Teresa of Calcutta liked to remind us, God will not judge us on the basis of how much we know or how right we have been. He will judge us by how much love we showed to others — particularly to the poor and forgotten in our midst. "Small things with great love," Mother Teresa used to tell her sisters.

Exhibiting her own humility, Mother Teresa used to keep her awards (including the Nobel Peace Prize of 1979) in a dusty cardboard box hidden atop a wardrobe in the corner of her bedroom. Instead of looking at her awards and polishing them each day, she looked at the poor and sick of India's worst slums, cleaning them with her own hands. God's love doesn't get much closer than that.

Accompanying and Listening

Pope Francis found his own maternal model of faith in his Grandmother Rosa, who took him to Holy Week devotions and prayed with him. By accompanying him at key moments of his childhood, this holy woman evangelized the future pope and brought him closer to God.

If we are willing to walk closely with our own family members and friends in this same way, listening rather than being too busy for them, we can make that kind of difference ourselves, like the mother who cares for her autistic daughter well beyond her own retirement age. Or the unmarried brother and sister who live with their infirm father well into their 40s, taking care of him at the expense of their own interests.

Jesus calls us to be with others, not fix their problems to make them go away. Francis writes movingly of this need for accompaniment:

> In our world, ordained ministers and other pastoral workers can make present the fragrance of Christ's closeness and his personal gaze. The Church will have to initiate everyone — priests, religious and laity — into this "art of accompaniment" which teaches us to remove our sandals before the sacred ground of the other (cf. Ex 3:5).
>
> The pace of this accompaniment must be steady and reassuring, reflecting our closeness and our compassionate gaze which also heals, liberates and encourages growth in the Christian life. (*Evangelii Gaudium* 169)

We need only a little willpower to enter into the messiness of people's lives, becoming close by accompanying and listening to them. Take, for example, Helen Keller's visually impaired teacher Anne Sullivan. She became the lifelong teacher and companion to this blind and deaf girl, thereby proving that the blind really *can* lead the blind.

If we have been victimized by family members or others in our lives, our wounds will give us good reason for staying away from them, as we must care for ourselves before we care for others. But if we form the habit of being so stuck in ourselves that we can only see our own problems and needs, Francis suggests our blindness to the reality of others will hurt more than it helps. He thus encourages us to ask God if we are truly accompanying the needy in our lives or keeping them at an unnecessary distance.

When we see others suffering, for instance, do we secretly rejoice that we are not like them? Or do we empathize with them? Do we feel compassion for the needy or despise them for their demands on us?

Do we spend time praying for and rejoicing and suffering with others, listening to them and walking with them closely regardless of our personal differences? Or do we pull back when the needs of the weak make us uncomfortable, preferring to fight our fellow Catholics in an ongoing struggle for power and control in the Church?

St. John Paul II, in an iconic moment of his papacy, visited Rebibbia prison on December 27, 1983, to pray silently with the Turkish hit man who shot him in St. Peter's Square on May 13, 1981. Overcome by emotion as he sat next to Mehmet Ali Agca, praying with him for forgiveness, John Paul II clutched the prisoner's arm with one hand and put the other hand to his own head.

Closeness requires this sort of open mind and open heart. To accompany people on the margins, we must be able to listen rather than lecture, opening ourselves to others. Francis writes:

> Listening, in communication, is an openness of heart which makes possible that closeness without which genuine spiritual encounter cannot occur. Listening helps us to find the right gesture and word which shows that we are more than simply bystanders.
>
> Only through such respectful and compassionate listening can we enter on the paths of true growth and awaken a yearning for the Christian ideal: the desire to respond fully to God's love and to bring to fruition what he has sown in our lives. (*Evangelii Gaudium* 171)

St. John Vianney, the Curé of Ars who spent most of his priestly life in the confessional, gives us another example of how to listen with compassion and patience to the needy around us.

A simple parish priest, Vianney drew thousands of people from faraway places to his rural confessional, where the lines rarely stopped. Rather than go out to distant lands in search of converts, he attracted people from all social sectors to his parish church with his ability to listen to them compassionately. By accompanying his penitents in the sacrament of God's mercy, Vianney drew them closer to God.

When Francis proclaimed a Year of Mercy for the Catholic Church beginning in Advent 2015, he didn't just hearken back to his coat of arms or vocation story rooted in the call of St. Matthew. He also reinforced the need for us to accompany others as God accompanies us.

Solidarity with All

Rather than rejoice that I am not like the needy and broken sinners who fill the world outside of my church, as the proud Pharisee did in the parable in Luke 18:9–14, Pope Francis asks me to pray for God's mercy as the tax collector did in the same story: "O God, be merciful to me a sinner."

To admit that I am like everyone else, rather than unique among all men on earth in my triumphs and flaws, requires a basic willingness to walk with others in solidarity — a prayerful awareness that we are all "in it together" on this planet and that we cannot journey to God on our own. And this solidarity — this closeness to God in companionship with the least and with all — requires our constant practice of humility, a virtue that St. Ignatius famously quipped "has never been sufficiently praised."

Jesus says in the Gospel of Matthew that "by their fruits you will know" those who follow God and those who do not (7:16). If we haven't washed each other's feet in this life, as we do symbolically on Holy Thursday, it's hard to imagine how God will recognize us in the afterlife. And if we haven't looked our suffering neighbors in the eye with compassion, accompanying their lives with genuine empathy, it's hard to imagine how we can ever see God face to face. As Jesus also tells us in the Gospel of Matthew, whoever is close to the least of our brothers and sisters in this life, will be close to him — and to them — in the next (25:40).

CHAPTER THREE

DIGNITY

When we live out a spirituality of drawing nearer to others and seeking their welfare, our hearts are opened wide to the Lord's greatest and most beautiful gifts.

Whenever we encounter another person in love, we learn something new about God. Whenever our eyes are opened to acknowledge the other, we grow in the light of faith and knowledge of God. (Evangelii Gaudium *272*)

Ashley sat on the sidewalk outside of Starbucks every afternoon with a cardboard sign, begging for money. She wore the same clothes every day. Sometimes people bought her something or gave her a few dollars. Most kept walking.

It was a typically hot New York summer in 2014. I was working at *America* magazine, the national Catholic review published by the Jesuits, and our Manhattan office was catty-corner to Ashley's perch. A twenty-three-year-old homeless woman, Ashley was one of thousands I saw begging on the streets around Fifth Avenue, and one of many suffering from mental illness and drug addiction.

Never in my life had I seen so many homeless people in one place before. I encountered them on walks to St. Patrick Cathedral, to coffee shops, and to the drugstore. They were everywhere.

I later learned from a social worker that homeless people from around the nation flock to Manhattan to score big money from tourists.

After a few days on the job, I found it hard to walk past these street people without engaging them — and it was especially hard for me to ignore Ashley as she sat for hours each day in front of a coffee shop that I often visited.

Whether or not I happened to be wearing my Jesuit clerical attire, I felt bad about sitting in the coffee shop and reading a book while people sat outside in misery. I also started to feel curious about them. What were they like? And what would I learn if I engaged them somehow?

Like most Catholics, I was faced anew with an even more basic moral question: What should I do when I pass a homeless person on the sidewalk? For much of my life, I've answered that question by simply staring straight ahead of me and continuing to walk. Unwilling to feed people's drug habits by giving them money, I only gave them food or food cards, or referred them to local homeless shelters.

My attitude started to change in July 2002, when I was crossing the Franz Joseph Bridge in Budapest with my grandfather during a summer visit to family. A worldly twenty-two-year-old college student, I started to walk deliberately past all of the beggars as we crossed this bridge over the Danube River, trying to avoid looking them in the eyes. But my grandfather, a Korean War veteran who had seen more of these things than I, suddenly pulled me up short in front of a legless man.

"You can't fake that," he told me, quietly pressing some Hungarian money into the man's hands.

My grandfather died in 2011. But whenever I see a homeless person today, I remember the look in my grandfather's eye. And it makes me think.

The Morality of Almsgiving

During my philosophy studies at Loyola University Chicago from 2007 to 2010, I occasionally bought meals for homeless people.

Once I took a homeless man inside a Subway restaurant on Michigan Avenue, where he pitched a fit and almost got us ejected before calming down. My clerical collar saved us from getting tossed out, fortunately, and he ended up happily showing me his artwork while he ate a sandwich stuffed with a bizarre mixture of ingredients that made my stomach turn. (Mayonnaise doesn't mix very well with jalapenos, banana peppers, pickles, chipotle sauce, vinegar, and ranch dressing.) After graduating from Loyola with my M.A. in Applied Philosophy, the question of how to help the homeless continued to bother me.

While teaching at Jesuit High School of Tampa from 2010 to 2014, I sometimes joined the service club on its weekly trips to a county-run shelter and to a downtown interfaith ministry, making and serving meals for the homeless in both places. One day, a homeless man who had attended a Jesuit university spooked some of my students by praising Jesuit education and giving them advice about college. Shrinking away, the kids seemed to fear that following his advice might lead them to catch homelessness themselves, as it if were a contagious disease.

Later, at the Jesuit School of Theology of Santa Clara University in spring 2015, my moral theology class discussed the question of what to do for a homeless person. Fr. Ed Krasevac, O.P., the Dominican friar who taught our class, used the example of panhandlers at Cheese Board Pizza in downtown Berkeley — a popular restaurant that he said offered the best sourdough bread in the world.

Fr. Krasevac noted that homeless people tend to hang out in front of Cheese Board, asking for people's pizza money while they wait in the long line each day. Do I give my $5 gourmet pizza money to them, Fr. Krasevac asked, or do I keep it? To the extent I think about Jesus and the Gospel, giving them the money is a good thing. But at the same time, it's also a bad thing because it deprives me of my lunch, which I have a reasonable expectation to enjoy each day.

In Thomist terms, Fr. Krasevac said the homeless person who asks for my money puts my intellect and will into a dynamic interaction with each other, setting the rational good (to give) against the sensible good (pizza) in a concrete situation. To give the money is a *sense* evil (no lunch), while not to give is a *rational* evil (no charity). What should I do?

Within the Catholic moral tradition, the purely intellectual view of giving the $5 away because almsgiving is objectively "good in itself" (and I had a big breakfast) is not enough to make it a good action, as I also need to understand subjectively that it's "good for me." Since I have a legitimate right to be happy, I must hook up the proposed action to my own sense of happiness.

We don't neglect to do good things for lack of will, Fr. Krasevac concluded, but for lack of knowing that they are good *for us.*

Emphasizing the same point, Pope Francis notes that Catholic moral teaching summons us primarily to a virtuous life of Gospel happiness or joy, not to a life of fearful obligation. The pope writes:

> Before all else, the Gospel invites us to respond to the God of love who saves us, to see God in others and to go forth from ourselves to seek the good of others. Under no circumstance can this invitation be obscured!
>
> All of the virtues are at the service of this response of love. If this invitation does not radiate forcefully and attractively, the edifice of the Church's moral teaching risks becoming a house of cards, and this is our greatest risk. (*Evangelii Gaudium* 39)

Francis emphasizes here that the morality of our actions depends on our intentions. The challenge remains, of course, to respond to Christ's call freely in a way that affirms the dignity of others. If we have never personally tried to engage a person in need, how can moral theology possibly help us?

When many of us see a homeless person or struggling immigrant in the United States, we quietly tell ourselves "not my problem" and keep walking. Pope Francis urges us to do otherwise.

Ashley's Story

While moral theology can teach us much about almsgiving, it can also help us rationalize our inactivity, and Pope Francis insists that nothing substitutes for direct contact with people on the margins. When push comes to shove, life experience trumps book learning.

During my summer in Manhattan, I sought to learn by experience how I might best relate to the homeless. Soon I started taking daily walks with food in my backpack, stopping to give things away and chat with any street people I came across on my way to Mass and other places. While making these rounds, I gradually got to know Ashley and her story, sitting down with her for regular talks.

Ashley told me her mother had died of cancer, and she had moved from her boyfriend's home to the streets after he became physically abusive. Because New York's homeless shelters didn't allow overnight guests to bring drugs with them, Ashley was begging on the streets to pay the nightly rent at a flophouse and to support her drug habit. On nights when she didn't make forty dollars to stay in the hostel, she slept on the subway, where she felt safest from violent attackers.

Optimistic that Ashley might want help due to her short time on the streets, I offered her resources for getting free medical screening and other social services. A Jesuit priest in

Chicago who works with the homeless gave me some guidance by telephone and email.

Unfortunately, the depths of Ashley's addictions and psychological traumas proved strong obstacles. In trying to connect Ashley with mental health services, I found it hard to make progress because she was too paranoid to trust public institutions. She was also too attached to her drug habit to grasp the reality that she would die on the streets if she stayed there.

On the positive side, she liked me and recognized that I wanted to help her. Ashley, who said she was raised Catholic, also seemed to trust me because I was a Catholic seminarian in a Roman collar. That basic trust allowed her to gradually open up and tell me more of her story.

She admitted to having psychological issues and to being from a family of meth addicts, some of whom had served jail time, but she said she had never received any treatment or medication. Ashley valued self-reliance, thinking she only had to get a job and make some money to solve all of her problems. She had deeply settled opinions on life, as well as strong feelings of guilt and self-condemnation for her inability to get off the streets.

Ashley sometimes prayed with me during our five- to ten-minute daily visits. But she also expressed toxic anger toward her family, boyfriend, God, and herself. Gradually, I realized the sad truth that I was not going to help her overcome homelessness.

In the final week of my daily visits with her, I turned the focus of our conversations to God, the invisible third presence on the streets. While Ashley knew that I was concerned and cared about her, I told her it was more important that God loved her and was present with her in her darkest moments.

On the day before I left New York, I entrusted Ashley to God, asking her to stand up and say good-bye properly with a hug in our final meeting.

I encouraged her to ask God to help her see the reality of her situation, to realize that she would die on the streets if she stayed there, to see that the "bad drugs" were blinding her to reality rather than helping her cope with it in a healthy way, to realize that she needed "good drugs" to overcome her psychological fears, and to ask God to help her see what she needed to do to turn her life around.

"God loves you and wants you to get off the streets," I told her. "Trust in God's love."

Although I didn't succeed in getting Ashley off the streets, I learned a lot about human dignity from her. It was often a painful experience, and the result wasn't ideal. But I hoped my efforts to affirm Ashley's dignity extended a lifeline she would one day pursue.

Life Lessons

Ethically, the biggest challenge of my summer in Manhattan was to help Ashley regain her sense of human dignity and place in society by inviting her take some small step toward healing.

In the beginning, I worked to build a trusting relationship by treating Ashley with great respect and clear boundaries. As I learned how to do so, I found it important to call her by her first name and ask her to use mine, to offer her the chance to pray with me, and to bring her food whenever she wanted it.

Quite often, I found that just looking a homeless person like Ashley in the eye and talking to her as I would to a friend or colleague was a great first step. They aren't used to being taken seriously.

While I did not give Ashley money, I worked to establish a supportive friendship based on mutual trust, and I also trusted her with some basic information about myself to build that trust. As I created this foundation of trust, I started bringing

Ashley information on local shelters for battered and homeless women, as well as information on the Homeless Coalition.

Of course she resisted all of these options, insisting that she alone could help herself escape the streets by getting a job. She claimed to be looking for work each week, but I saw no evidence that she was actually applying for jobs as often as she claimed.

On some days, she looked terrible and seemed completely out of it, high on some kind of street drugs. She didn't want to admit that her coping mechanisms weren't working or that the drugs were actually making her situation worse by blinding her to the terrifying reality of life on the streets.

Another lesson I learned was that getting close to her wasn't easy. She was often paranoid. Sometimes the genuineness of my concern for her made her feel worse about her situation.

Still, Ashley kept the resources I gave her and promised to think about getting help. I even wrote her a farewell note, enclosing a Sacred Heart of Jesus badge from the Apostleship of Prayer to give her a sacramental reminder of our discussions and of her relationship with God.

Though I was saddened that Ashley hadn't left the streets by the time I departed from my summer assignment, I prayed that our friendship somehow planted a seed of grace for her return to society.

In the end, I learned three broad lessons from working with Ashley. First, that the best thing I could do for homeless persons as a Catholic was to treat them with respect and dignity, hoping for the best while expecting nothing. Second, that God exists and has the power to save people if they let him. Third, that I am not God.

Even in the affluent United States, all of us deal with the homeless at some point in our lives, and all of us must discern how to respond to them.

It's not easy, and there's no simple answer. Street people remind us of the margins to which Christ calls us. Their very existence scandalizes our economy and invites us to do more than what we find comfortable.

But even the Holy Family (Jesus, Mary, and Joseph) found itself homeless as it fled King Herod's soldiers into Egypt.

Pope Francis, in his insistence that every person is worthy of our giving, has often noted that we must see *ourselves* in the needy before we can really see Christ there. He notes that when we refuse to acknowledge our own homelessness as finite creatures, we find it easier to drift away from God and forget our common human dignity:

> Some people think they are free if they can avoid God; they fail to see that they remain existentially orphaned, helpless, homeless. They cease being pilgrims and become drifters, flitting around themselves and never getting anywhere. (*Evangelii Gaudium* 170)

While many ordinary Catholics may fear that engaging the homeless is too much for us, Francis urges the entire Church to do so.

Just as forcefully, he also encourages us to engage the illegal immigrants and the elderly in our midst, whose existence we may likewise ignore despite its proximity to our daily lives. Francis writes:

> It is essential to draw near to new forms of poverty and vulnerability, in which we are called to recognize the suffering Christ, even if this appears to bring us no tangible and immediate benefits.
>
> I think of the homeless, the addicted, refugees, indigenous peoples, the elderly who are increasingly isolated and abandoned, and many others. Migrants present a particular challenge for me, since I am the

pastor of a Church without frontiers, a Church which considers herself mother to all. (*Evangelii Gaudium* 210)

To go to the margins, then, means to love others with a closeness that builds up their dignity. As Christians, we cannot in good conscience ignore such people without feeling bothered. Whether we are dealing with the homeless person on the street corner, the undocumented worker at our job, or the elderly person in our own family, Jesus calls us to learn new ways to affirm their inherent dignity as fellow human beings equal in God's eyes.

Meeting the Elderly

Unfortunately, there are many things in our world to distract us from the dignity of people on the margins, even when they live right next door to us.

Pope Francis is particularly concerned for the elderly who increasingly are treated like "trash," as he memorably said in a speech to the Pontifical Commission for Latin America:

> I remember visiting a retirement home for the elderly in Buenos Aires, which belonged to the State. The beds were all occupied; so they were putting mattresses on the floor, and the elderly just lay there. A country cannot buy a bed? This is indicative of something else, is it not? They are like waste material. Soiled sheets, with every sort of filth; without a napkin and the poor old people were eating there, they were wiping their mouths with the sheet…. I saw this with my own eyes, no one told me about it. They are treated like trash.

In his own life at the Vatican, Pope Francis's affection for Pope Benedict in some way captures his perspective on the dignity and inherent value of those whose more productive years are behind them. While some newspapers have speculated about the power dynamics of "two popes in the Vatican," Francis has cheerfully likened the situation to living with "Grandpa."

On the night of Pope Francis's election, when much of the world had forgotten about the retired Benedict XVI, a funny thing happened between these two popes behind the scenes. Wanting to show respect for his predecessor, Francis insisted on calling Benedict to give him the results of the papal election before revealing himself to the world. So while the crowd waited an unusually long time for the new pope to walk out onto the balcony overlooking St. Peter's Square, Francis was actually trying to reach Benedict on the phone.

Benedict, sitting before a television in the papal summer residence at Castel Gandolfo a few miles away, ignored the ringing telephone. He didn't want to miss the first appearance of the new pope by getting up to answer the phone!

Eventually, the Vatican reached a worker at Castel Gandolfo, who got word to Benedict that the new pope was trying to call him. After speaking for a few minutes with Benedict on the phone, Pope Francis finally emerged into the night sky to reveal himself to the world. Standing at his balcony, Francis then asked the crowd to pray for his predecessor, leading the assembled faithful in a Hail Mary for Benedict.

By honoring Benedict in this way and including him in the events of that night, Francis quietly demonstrated that the "economy of exclusion" that throws away old people as unproductive has no place in the Gospel.

The deep esteem Francis has continued to show toward Benedict is not based on what he can "get" from the retired pope or on what Grandpa can "do" for him. It is not motivated by guilt or obligation. Rather, it is rooted in Francis's deeply felt conviction that all of us have dignity from God, which nothing can take away. Francis contrasts this Christian view with our "throw away" culture in *The Joy of the Gospel*:

Human beings are themselves considered consumer goods to be used and then discarded. We have created a "throw away" culture which is now spreading. It is no longer simply about exploitation and oppression, but something new.

Exclusion ultimately has to do with what it means to be a part of the society in which we live; those excluded are no longer society's underside or its fringes or its disenfranchised — they are no longer even a part of it. The excluded are not the "exploited" but the outcast, the "leftovers." (*Evangelii Gaudium* 53)

All of us, if we pray about it, can do *something* to recognize the dignity of the outcast and excluded, the homeless person we pass on the way to work or the elderly relative sitting alone in a nursing home. And that is precisely Francis's point.

Getting Involved

No matter what we choose to do, Francis invites us to do *something*.

Many of our Catholic parishes help the needy through the St. Vincent de Paul Society and other social outreach ministries. Even if we do not have time to volunteer, we can pray for and support these ministries financially.

As citizens of the United States, lay Catholics also have the freedom to fight for recognition of the marginalized through political action that transforms charity into justice. Francis writes:

This means education, access to health care, and above all employment, for it is through free, creative, participatory and mutually supportive labor that human beings express and enhance the dignity of their lives. A just wage enables them to have adequate access to all the other goods which are destined for our common use. (*Evangelii Gaudium* 192)

Each of us can learn and apply Catholic social teaching in some small way and work to improve the status quo by changing hearts and minds one person at a time.

Dorothy Day and Peter Maurin, two laypeople who cofounded the Catholic Worker Movement in New York City in the 1930s, tried to change the status quo by creating "houses of hospitality" to care for the poor and homeless. They also started a newspaper, *The Catholic Worker*, to advocate for a living wage and other public policies on behalf of the excluded.

A former Communist journalist who converted to Catholicism upon recognizing it as the religion of the poor, Day came to God after two failed relationships resulted in an abortion and a daughter born out of wedlock. Resurrected as a Catholic radical, she faced opposition from atheists and churchgoers alike for her relentless focus on street people — to the point that Cardinal Francis Spellman asked her in 1951 to consider removing the word "Catholic" from her group's name. (Day respectfully but firmly refused.)

Nevertheless, other Catholics did support Day's movement and have continued to do so. Today she is a Servant of God and Cardinal Timothy Dolan, Spellman's successor in the Archdiocese of New York, is promoting her cause for canonization. At their annual fall meeting in Baltimore in 2012, the U.S. bishops endorsed this same cause in a voice vote.

Day, who led a deep prayer life as a Benedictine oblate and died in 1980 at the age of eighty-three, never sought this recognition. "Don't call me a saint," she once quipped. "I don't want to be dismissed so easily."

Mistrusted by critics who during her lifetime didn't like being reminded of poor people's dignity, Day has ironically become a prophetic role model for American Catholics in her death.

As we go to the margins ourselves, Francis says we will continue to face such opposition from people who aren't ready to go there with us. He writes:

> The dignity of each human person and the pursuit of the common good are concerns which ought to shape all economic policies. At times, however, they seem to be a mere addendum imported from without in order to fill out a political discourse lacking in perspectives or plans for true and integral development.
>
> How many words prove irksome to this system! It is irksome when the question of ethics is raised, when global solidarity is invoked, when the distribution of goods is mentioned, when reference is made to protecting labor and defending the dignity of the powerless, when allusion is made to a God who demands a commitment to justice. (*Evangelii Gaudium* 203)

Francis knows that our politicians often resist systemic efforts to affirm the dignity of the poor, preferring a rhetoric that justifies selfish or immoral policies by appealing to concern for the needy. But in response to this reality, the pope calls on Christians themselves to witness to the dignity of excluded people through political action as well as direct charity. In a section recalling the Ignatian maxim that love expresses itself more fully in deeds than in words, Francis elaborates on what happens to a church that forgets this prophetic calling:

> Any Church community, if it thinks it can comfortably go its own way without creative concern and effective cooperation in helping the poor to live with dignity and reaching out to everyone, will also risk

breaking down, however much it may talk about social issues or criticize governments. It will easily drift into a spiritual worldliness camouflaged by religious practices, unproductive meetings and empty talk. (*Evangelii Gaudium* 207)

Besides the homeless and the elderly, Francis encourages us to recognize the dignity of the unborn, supporting pro-life policies and reaching out to help unwed mothers.

When it comes to pro-life issues, Francis defies political leftists who favor legal abortion, just as he alienates political conservatives with his opposition to unbridled capitalism. But for the pope, unborn children remain the neediest of all human beings. He writes:

Among the vulnerable for whom the Church wishes to care with particular love and concern are unborn children, the most defenseless and innocent among us. Nowadays efforts are made to deny them their human dignity and to do with them whatever one pleases, taking their lives and passing laws preventing anyone from standing in the way of this.

Frequently, as a way of ridiculing the Church's effort to defend their lives, attempts are made to present her position as ideological, obscurantist and conservative. Yet this defense of unborn life is closely linked to the defense of each and every other human right. (*Evangelii Gaudium* 213)

On this issue as on others, Francis doesn't tell us *how* to go out to the margins, but exhorts us to pray and work for God's kingdom in whatever way makes the biggest impact. Regardless of how we choose to support the dignity of the needy, our evangelization must lead us into a deepening relationship with God that allows us to be leaven in the world, helping to build his kingdom.

Learning about God

As we go out of our comfort zone, Francis foresees we will grow in our personal faith and knowledge of God.

I have experienced this humbling grace many times in my own religious life. When I was a Jesuit novice, my fellow novices and I made weekly visits to two nursing homes in rural Louisiana, spending time with people whose families rarely visited them.

Many of these folks, suffering from Alzheimer's and other ailments, often told the same stories over and over again. We listened, played bingo, and prayed with them.

Our visits usually cheered the mostly Catholic residents, who appreciated seeing young seminarians and felt lifted from their depression and loneliness by our interest in them.

"I can't stand that woman next to me," one lady confided to me every time I visited, smiling when she said it.

We also worked in hospitals and hospices where we prayed with the sick and dying and, in private, frequently recited the "Prayer for Generosity" of St. Ignatius, also known as the "Prayer of a Christian Soldier."

> Lord, teach me to be generous.
> Teach me to serve you as you deserve;
> to give and not to count the cost,
> to fight and not to heed the wounds,
> to toil and not to seek for rest,
> to labor and not to ask for reward,
> save that of knowing that I do your will.

One other experience comes to mind regarding the dignity of others regardless of their circumstances.

In the first year of my theology studies in Berkeley, I started working for the Catholic chaplaincy at San Quentin prison, attending Sunday Mass and visiting prisoners in their cells afterward.

Through this ministry, I had many pastoral conversations with prisoners in the reception center, death row, solitary confinement, and special protective custody — all men thrown away by our society in punishment for their crimes against it. Many of these guys had been locked up for thirty years or more.

On Easter Sunday 2015, I spent several hours visiting the inmates of one tier in the cell blocks after Mass. It was an emotionally draining experience, but deeply humbling to be in a position to comfort these men who couldn't call or speak to their families on the holiday.

"Thanks for spending Easter with us," one man told me through the bars of his cell. "You didn't have to be here today."

In treating these men with dignity and respect, I couldn't change their reality, but I was able to bring them comfort in a small way. Joined by a fellow Jesuit, I prayed with many men whose criminal records I preferred not to know.

One week later, I prayed briefly with a man in protective custody whose daughter was about to be taken off life support at a hospital in San Francisco just a few miles away.

Unable to leave the prison to be at her deathbed, the man was too grief-stricken to say more than a few words to me. For several minutes that felt like hours, I shared his grief in silence and held his hand. I then voiced a brief prayer for him and moved on.

As we learn about God from drawing closer to people on the margins in whatever way is available to us, Francis suggests we will find God himself in the dignity of the poor. And on the margins, Christ himself restores *our* dignity.

God Affirms Us

Flannery O'Connor, in her short story "The Displaced Person," tells the tale of a Polish immigrant who unintentionally stirs up racial bigotry in 1955 rural Georgia through his instinctive values of hard work and equal dignity for all.

This Mr. Guizac, whom the locals call a "D.P." because war has displaced him from Europe, works hard for low wages on a farm and tries to marry one of his family members to a black sharecropper. When his white employer Mrs. McIntyre finds out, she turns on the Pole and persecutes him.

With sneaky wit, O'Connor gives Mrs. McIntyre a memorable zinger as she complains in frustration to the priest who had asked her to hire Mr. Guizac: "As far as I'm concerned, Christ was just another D.P."

Ironically, Mrs. McIntyre is right.

Jesus Christ, God incarnate, was himself an immigrant whose family took him into Egypt to escape Herod's sword. Jesus was a migrant who received no honor as a prophet in his native place, becoming instead a homeless wanderer who preached to the needy.

The Gospels reinforce O'Connor's message that Jesus identified strongly with society's outcasts, enjoying their company rather than simply enduring it. He ate with sinners, tax collectors, and prostitutes. Rejected by the society he came to redeem, he died a shameful death.

Christ's life also reminds us that the only person from the Gospels whom we know for certain went to heaven was a convicted criminal.

In the Gospel of Luke, chapter 23, the good thief, known in Catholic tradition as St. Dismas, asks Jesus to remember him when he comes into his kingdom. Jesus responds by assuring him of a place in heaven, saying: "Amen, I say to you, today you will be with me in Paradise."

Penitent on the cross, St. Dismas confessed that he had lived a sinful life and received just punishment for his crimes. But Jesus looked at him with mercy and pardoned him, even in the midst of his own dying agony. The scribes and Pharisees undoubtedly despised Jesus even for this final act of mercy.

Such stories illustrate how Jesus himself was a man of the margins, ultimately forgotten and despised in his lifetime by most of those who knew him. Although he was innocent, he forgave a criminal who was not. He reached out to a man who was more like the convicts at San Quentin than the regular churchgoers of our own time.

These stories also reassure us that God's mercy is undeserved, affirming our human dignity when we least expect it, provided we keep our hearts open to receive him.

To recall the dream of a character in another O'Connor story, we may even find one day that we can recognize Jesus Christ in the people we judged most undesirable in our own neighborhoods, all hooting and hollering as they ascend to heaven.

He'll be there to welcome the crude and the ordinary, those the rest of us found too embarrassing to be around. He'll see the dignity in those we neglected, while we — the people of "good order, and common sense and respectable behavior," as O'Connor puts it in her short story "A Temple of the Holy Ghost" — might find ourselves relegated to the rear of the procession, as even our "virtues" are "burned away."

At another point in this same story, two Catholic schoolgirls joke to a younger girl about how Sister Perpetua has advised them to defend themselves against starry-eyed boys by saying, "Stop sir! I am a Temple of the Holy Ghost!"

Ironically, this phrase becomes real by the end of the story, as the young girl imagines a hermaphrodite circus performer at the local "freak show" repeating it as a prayer.

"I am a Temple of the Holy Ghost, Amen."

And so are we all — rich and poor, powerful and weak.

CHAPTER FOUR

WEARINESS

We all know from experience that sometimes a task does not bring the satisfaction we seek, results are few and changes are slow, and we are tempted to grow weary. Yet lowering our arms momentarily out of weariness is not the same as lowering them for good, overcome by chronic discontent and by a listlessness that parches the soul.

It also happens that our hearts can tire of the struggle because in the end we are caught up in ourselves, in a careerism which thirsts for recognition, applause, rewards and status. In this case we do not lower our arms, but we no longer grasp what we seek, the resurrection is not there. In cases like these, the Gospel, the most beautiful message that this world can offer, is buried under a pile of excuses. (Evangelii Gaudium *277*)

Ugh. Another twelve-hour workday is staring me in the face.

Dragging myself out of bed at 6:30 a.m., I move in a fog to the shower, telling myself out loud: "It's going to be a great day!"

They say positive thinking helps. I'm not sure who "they" are, but it seems legit.

After shaving in the dark, I throw my chain of religious medals over my neck, put on my faded black clerical shirt, and insert a white plastic Roman collar into the neckband.

It might sound like I'm Batman, but I'm not. Batman doesn't ache this much when he gets out of bed.

As I put my shoes on, I glance at the daily Scripture readings for Mass and try to remember a key phrase for private reflection throughout the day. Picking up an armful of papers and a clipboard, I mutter a prayer and leave my room.

Then without wasting time, I go downstairs, eat breakfast standing up in the kitchen, and finally leave the Jesuit residence to walk over to the high school campus next door. In the chapel, I take homeroom attendance just before our daily convocation prayer service with 750 students and faculty.

I teach from 8:00 a.m. to 3:30 p.m., meet students after school, overwork to get off campus by 4:00, go home to the Jesuit residence, and unintentionally fall asleep in my easy chair while praying.

In the classroom each day, I am a cross between entertainer and train conductor. I keep things moving, solve countless minor crises, and support the students in myriad ways. Some kids laugh at my jokes and appear to think I might be a superhero after all. Others find me boring. I'm not sure I care what they think either way.

Between classes and proctoring duties, I occasionally have five minutes to get a cup of coffee or use the restroom before reporting to my next period. During the day I have one free period, less than an hour long, to prep classes and catch up on grading.

Later I attend a Jesuit community Mass at 5:00 p.m., community vespers at 5:30, dinner at 6:00, and a sporting event after dinner. Following the game, I come home to grade papers again. On nights when there is no sporting event, I find time to watch a little television or go out for a cup of coffee with another Jesuit after dinner. Most nights, I don't have this luxury.

Come morning, I will start the whole routine over again. There's nothing in the world quite like religious life at a Jesuit prep school.

The Depths of Fatigue

For four straight years, this routine was my life in Tampa, Florida, five days a week. There was little variation in the schedule and no other way to proceed. I could either teach or quit my Jesuit vocation, but I couldn't do both.

Weekends were likewise full of school events, requiring me to drive students on trips or show up to assist at various liturgies and other events. I played my trombone with the school band and coached the speech and debate team, spending many long weekends at high school forensics tournaments.

Prayer was important to me, but I had little time for it outside of the prayer that was my work.

In all my life, I've rarely been more tired than I was teaching high school, and for the most part I was never happier to be so tired. But there were days. Oh yes, there were days.

In my first year, a spirited group of juniors nearly destroyed me, throwing their inexperienced teacher into desolation. Unsure of what to do, I tried talking over them and strained my vocal chords.

Being a Jesuit seminarian in a Roman collar gave me no protection. If anything, it made things worse, sometimes giving me the impression that I was walking around with a big "sucker" sign on my back.

It didn't take long for me to break. Near the end of month one, I lost my voice for several days, reaching the point where I couldn't make any sound at all.

On the first day of this imposed silence, I fooled two freshman classes by putting my finger to my lips as they entered the room and pointing to the dry-erase board, where I had posted a quiz. Somehow they took the quiz and left without realizing I couldn't talk. I felt miserable.

At one point later that fall, I went four straight weeks without leaving campus. I was so busy with class prep and grading that I didn't have time for anything else.

By year two, I had learned to control my classroom, and the boys enjoyed my theology class. By year three, I didn't have to yell at all. I was also coordinating the school's sixty altar servers, making sure the guys didn't burn down the chapel at school Masses with the incense and thurible. I had learned to practice a deeper awareness of Christ's presence during the day and to make the most of my after-school meditation, however brief it was at times.

Reaching my fourth and final year of teaching, I had achieved personal balance and become a trusted faculty member, but the work had taken its toll on me. I had reached the point of burnout that all well-meaning Catholics eventually hit in ministry. Alert to this danger, I realized I had to ease up on my commitments and say "no" to a few things during that final year, or else I would be doing a disservice both to myself and to the kids I was serving.

Facing Burnout

During the fall semester of my last year at the high school, I was deeply touched to read in the pope's apostolic exhortation that Catholics who go out to the margins need to be honest with ourselves about fatigue and burnout — not in a guilt-inducing way, but with an energy and compassion that stays rooted in the Gospel joy we have received from Jesus.

Commenting on the dangers of weariness, Francis writes:

> Sometimes we lose our enthusiasm for mission because we forget that the Gospel responds to our deepest needs, since we were created for what the Gospel offers us: friendship with Jesus and love of our brothers and sisters. (*Evangelii Gaudium* 265)

Admittedly, "sometimes we lose our enthusiasm for mission" feels like a euphemism to anyone who has experienced ministry fatigue. Sometimes it's more accurate to admit to ourselves that we are just plain tired, overworked, and overwrought because we have neglected our own deepest needs in order to help others.

Not only priests, but all who work in helping professions are vulnerable to the physical and spiritual effects of fatigue. Social workers as well as those who volunteer in ministries to the poor often notice themselves feeling irritable, impatient, and resentful when they don't bother to care for themselves.

Emphasizing how healthy self-care requires us to stay focused on the reason for our evangelization, Francis notes that our ability to endure weariness depends on our ability to sense Christ's supportive presence in our daily lives. He writes:

> It is impossible to persevere in a fervent evangelization unless we are convinced from personal experience that it is not the same thing to have known Jesus as not to have known him, not the same thing to walk with him as to walk blindly, not the same thing to hear his word as not to know it, and not the same thing to contemplate him, to worship him, to find our peace in him, as not to. It is not the same thing to try to build the world with his Gospel as to try to do so by our own lights.
>
> We know well that with Jesus life becomes richer and that with him it is easier to find meaning in everything. This is why we evangelize. A true missionary, who never ceases to be a disciple, knows that Jesus walks with him, speaks to him, breathes with him, works with him. He senses Jesus alive with him in the midst of the missionary enterprise. Unless we see him present at the heart of our missionary commitment, our enthusiasm soon wanes and we are no longer sure

of what it is that we are handing on; we lack vigor and passion. (*Evangelii Gaudium* 266)

In ministry, Francis says the cure for our weariness is clear: We must continually direct our thoughts, feelings, prayers, and awareness to the sustaining presence of Jesus Christ in our daily lives. If we fail to do so, turning our attention to things other than Jesus, we will soon stop following him. As I had learned for myself in the high school, this truth is not a flowery sentiment, but the daily reality of all who labor successfully in God's vineyard for very long.

Jesus himself knew disciples who left him after an early period of excitement. In the Gospels, we read about the "would-be followers of Jesus" who begin to tire of the mission when it gets too demanding, making excuses to the Messiah for their sudden decision to leave (see Lk 9:57–62; Mt 8:18–22).

One man in this story promises to follow Jesus but seems uncertain about it, prompting the Lord to admit up front that weariness awaits anyone who shares his life. Jesus tells the man: "Foxes have dens and birds of the sky have nests, but the Son of Man has nowhere to rest his head" (Mt 8:20).

For those of us who work or volunteer in Catholic ministries today, it might sometimes be helpful to give this sort of disclaimer up front, allowing an "out" for would-be colleagues who aren't deeply committed to evangelization. "Birds have nests, but Directors of Religious Education have no time to relax," we might tell our applicants for a job opening at the local parish.

At some point, all of us have met evangelizers who thought they knew what they were getting into but later found the reality of daily "church work" too difficult to sustain. I certainly saw a lot of teachers come and go at Jesuit High School.

"I thought I wanted to teach in a Catholic school, but the students here drive me crazy," one of them told me shortly before leaving. "I'm going to find another career."

Speaking of today's would-be disciples, Pope Francis writes:

> Called to radiate light and communicate life, in the end they are caught up in things that generate only darkness and inner weariness, and slowly consume all zeal for the apostolate. For all this, I repeat: Let us not allow ourselves to be robbed of the joy of evangelization! (*Evangelii Gaudium* 83)

To show up for one's ministry each day, ready and eager to evangelize, requires an inner victory over the demon that tempts us to self-seeking despair. Focusing on worldly achievements, rather than on Jesus, discourages us from evangelizing. Without a sense of meaning and purpose in our missionary activity, supported by a lively companionship with Jesus in prayer, it becomes impossible to sustain a lasting commitment to the needy.

Francis elaborates on this point:

> What is needed is the ability to cultivate an interior space which can give a Christian meaning to commitment and activity. Without prolonged moments of adoration, of prayerful encounter with the word, of sincere conversation with the Lord, our work easily becomes meaningless; we lose energy as a result of weariness and difficulties, and our fervor dies out.
>
> The Church urgently needs the deep breath of prayer, and to my great joy groups devoted to prayer and intercession, the prayerful reading of God's word and the perpetual adoration of the Eucharist are growing at every level of ecclesial life.
>
> Even so, "we must reject the temptation to offer a privatized and individualistic spirituality which ill

accords with the demands of charity, to say nothing of the implications of the incarnation" (John Paul II, *Novo Millennio Inuente*, 52). There is always the risk that some moments of prayer can become an excuse for not offering one's life in mission; a privatized lifestyle can lead Christians to take refuge in some false forms of spirituality. (*Evangelii Gaudium* 262)

Francis suggests that if we try to work on the margins as isolated individuals without a strong prayer life, we will inevitably become exhausted and turn to other pursuits as our enthusiasm fades. But prayer can save us. We can fight to keep our fervor alive by establishing a daily personal prayer time, joining a prayer group, reading Scripture, participating in Eucharistic adoration, and seeking out other opportunities for prayerful encounters with Jesus.

While a healthy self-love is necessary for us to love others with empathy, we must remain rooted more deeply in our prayerful awareness of Christ's presence — and of our solidarity with other evangelizers — to resist the fatal attitude that self-sacrifice is meaningless. Francis writes:

Some people do not commit themselves to mission because they think that nothing will change and that it is useless to make the effort. They think: "Why should I deny myself my comforts and pleasures if I won't see any significant result?" This attitude makes it impossible to be a missionary. (*Evangelii Gaudium* 275)

Many of us have experienced, in ourselves and in others, the ways that this kind of reasoning can erode a sincere missionary commitment to Jesus Christ. We may have grown up with Catholic friends who spent their high school and college years as leaders in campus ministry only to leave it — as well as the Church — when they found something else to occupy their time. They were the first to show up for Eucharistic adoration and other devotions in school but gradually fell away because their spirituality remained disconnected from their relationships.

We may have also known young Catholics who spent themselves tirelessly in social justice ministries for a year or two, reveling in shared anger against "the system." Once they realized they could not change the world overnight, they ended up taking well-paying jobs and buying expensive cars.

Such Catholics are invariably well-meaning, just as Christ's would-be followers had good intentions. But the deeper support they need to endure weariness and really make a difference is missing. As Francis reminds us, that support comes from growing in our relationships with Jesus and others through prayer.

Praying Generously

While private prayer is essential to a healthy spiritual life, Francis warns missionaries against using it to turn too far inward, coming to see themselves as isolated individuals who must either save the world or totally give up on it. Unable to ask others for help or to play well in the sandbox as part of an apostolic team, such people may pray to keep others at a distance rather than bring them close. Secret resentments and unmet needs distort their love of neighbor.

By contrast, Francis says the true disciple prays with generosity, seeking union with Jesus and others. That doesn't mean every prayer must occur in a group, but it does mean that all of us are called to contemplate Jesus and see the needs of others in our spiritual lives. Even when we pray alone, we can pray for and with others by uniting ourselves to their intentions rather than fixating on our personal successes and failures in an unhealthy way.

This commitment to other-centered prayer invites an attitude of self-giving that transcends weariness. In his *Suscipe* prayer, St. Ignatius of Loyola expresses this spirit of generosity in words dearly familiar to Pope Francis and all Jesuits. While various English translations of the original Latin text from the *Spiritual Exercises* exist, printed in back of the Roman Missal and elsewhere, I prefer my own version that I use in personal prayer:

> Receive, Lord, all my liberty.
> Take my memory, my understanding,
> and my entire will.
> All that I have and possess, you have given to me.
> To you, O Lord, I return it.
> Dispose of it wholly according to your will.
> Give me only your love and your grace,
> and I am rich enough and ask for nothing more.

This God-focused prayer has sustained six centuries of Jesuits, including Pope Francis, in weary mission work down to the present day. It is the prayer of every Jesuit who decides to offer his entire life in grateful return for all God has done for him. But it is also the prayer of every ordinary man or woman who discovers firsthand that God welcomes our love with delight — assuming we offer it freely out of genuine desire for the good of others and not out of compulsion.

Another prayer that Jesuits use in the spiritual battle against weariness is the Daily Offering for the monthly intentions of the Holy Father.

While the pope and the Society of Jesus promote these intentions annually through the Apostleship of Prayer, one needn't know them to simply offer Jesus the various ups and downs of the day in union with him and others. The traditional morning offering reads:

> O Jesus, through the Immaculate Heart of Mary, I
> offer you my prayers, works, joys, and sufferings of

this day in union with the holy sacrifice of the Mass throughout the world. I offer them for all the intentions of your Sacred Heart: the salvation of souls, reparation for sin, and the reunion of all Christians. I offer them for the intentions of our bishops and of all Apostles of Prayer, and in particular for those recommended by our Holy Father this month.

Even when we find ourselves confined to our homes by age or infirmity, we can unite our prayers with those of Pope Francis and the universal Church by reciting this simple daily offering. Such God-focused prayers help draw us out of our weary despair, uniting our hearts and minds in Jesus Christ.

It is this union that sustains us. Attentive to the human tendency to seek validation from the world rather than from Jesus, Francis insists again and again that God alone can relieve our fatigue:

> Sometimes it seems that our work is fruitless, but mission is not like a business transaction or investment, or even a humanitarian activity. It is not a show where we count how many people come as a result of our publicity; it is something much deeper, which escapes all measurement. It may be that the Lord uses our sacrifices to shower blessings in another part of the world which we will never visit.
>
> The Holy Spirit works as he wills, when he wills and where he wills; we entrust ourselves without pretending to see striking results. We know only that our commitment is necessary. Let us learn to rest in the tenderness of the arms of the Father amid our creative and generous commitment. Let us keep marching forward; let us give him everything, allowing him to make our efforts bear fruit in his good time. (*Evangelii Gaudium* 279)

In our ministry to the marginalized, Francis invites us to make room for God's loving presence as we strive to transcend our human need for results, acting instead out of the disinterested love that characterizes our greatest saints. If we have not matured beyond the youthful insecurity that drives us to seek a pat on the back for every good deed, and beyond our restless need for measurable successes, then we have not truly begun to be missionaries as Francis envisions us.

St. Ignatius was once reproached by his family during a visit home for wanting to teach catechism to poor children in town rather than stay at the castle. "Nobody will come," they told him, trying to discourage him from offering catechism lessons. Indignant, Ignatius shot back that even one soul would be enough — an infinite audience.

To keep Jesus Christ in the center is the only sure guide for all Christians who wish to go out to the margins as missionaries. Without appropriating Christ's total self-commitment on a deeply felt level, free of disordered self-love, one cannot possibly endure weariness for long.

The Miracle of Perseverance

Pope Francis has faced weariness many times in his own life. As archbishop of Buenos Aires, he battled with Argentine civil authorities over a governmental system that often flaunted wealth and power at the expense of the dispossessed masses and espoused values hostile to Christian life.

Yet Francis has persevered in his focus on Jesus, warning Christians to avoid gossip and other infighting that allows the Evil Spirit to thrive by turning our weariness into angry despair.

For Francis, weariness can become a pessimism that turns our eyes away from Christ's grace. He writes:

> One of the more serious temptations which stifles boldness and zeal is a defeatism which turns us into

querulous and disillusioned pessimists, "sourpusses." Nobody can go off to battle unless he is fully convinced of victory beforehand. If we start without confidence, we have already lost half the battle and we bury our talents. While painfully aware of our own frailties, we have to march on without giving in, keeping in mind what the Lord said to Saint Paul: "My grace is sufficient for you, for my power is made perfect in weakness" (2 Cor 12:9).

Christian triumph is always a cross, yet a cross which is at the same time a victorious banner borne with aggressive tenderness against the assaults of evil. The evil spirit of defeatism is brother to the temptation to separate, before its time, the wheat from the weeds; it is the fruit of an anxious and self-centered lack of trust. (*Evangelii Gaudium* 85)

While Francis identifies selfishness as the sinful root of the defeatism and lack of trust that flow from unrelieved weariness, he sees confident perseverance as the grace that helps us to overcome them. And perseverance, despite its lack of obvious supernatural roots, can be a miraculous gift.

St. Joseph Pignatelli, a Spanish Jesuit who lived from 1737 to 1811, offers one example of how perseverance in trials can bear fruit in miracles.

After Spain expelled the Society of Jesus from its domains in 1767, St. Joseph became a leader of hundreds of Spanish Jesuits exiled on the island of Sardinia. Europe's monarchs, gradually expelling the Jesuits in a unified political strike against the papacy, were dismantling the Society piece by piece at this time.

In some countries, Jesuits were allowed to leave the order peacefully, joining the diocesan clergy or forming new congregations. In other places, they were deported from their homelands or arrested and thrown into dungeons. Various governments seized Jesuit schools and Church properties, either closing them or giving them to other clergy to run.

But in the midst of all this chaos, Pignatelli refused to renounce his vows. He had entered the order at age fifteen, and he intended to die in it, even if he turned out to be the last Jesuit in the world.

In 1773, Pope Clement XIV issued a bull of universal suppression, disbanding the Society of Jesus. He also imprisoned Fr. Lorenzo Ricci, the Jesuit superior general, in Castel Sant'Angelo, where he died two years later.

Tens of thousands of Jesuits, and countless ministries in a missionary network spanning hundreds of countries, disappeared almost overnight.

At this point, with every opportunity to leave the imploding Jesuit order, Pignatelli refused. Many people said he was wrong to do so. But God had other plans for him.

In Russia, Queen Catherine the Great — a German Protestant — had chosen not to promulgate the papal bull of suppression because she liked the Jesuit schools in Lithuania and Poland. Ordering her Catholic bishops not to enforce the bull, she made it clear she did not accept the pope's authority in her realm.

Seeing this loophole, Pignatelli traveled to Russia to renew his vows with the couple of hundred Jesuits there who had survived the suppression — men who had continued running their few schools and parishes in confused obedience to Catherine.

For the next forty years, as subsequent popes quietly encouraged these Jesuits to endure and cautiously began to rebuild the Society, Pignatelli became a novice master and leader among the remnant. He worked to inspire and strengthen his men, keeping them focused on God's desires for them.

Throughout these long years, Pignatelli recited a daily prayer of perseverance that helped him endure the painful twists and turns of his life. His Christ-focused prayer reads:

My God, I do not know what must come to me today.
But I am certain that nothing can happen to me
that you have not foreseen, decreed, and ordained
from all eternity.
That is sufficient for me.
I adore your impenetrable and eternal designs,
to which I submit with all my heart.
I desire, I accept them all, and I unite my sacrifice
to that of Jesus Christ, my divine Savior.
I ask, in his name and through his infinite merits,
patience in my trials and perfect and entire submission
to all that comes to me by your good pleasure. Amen.

Although he dreamed of living to see the Society of Jesus restored throughout the world, St. Joseph Pignatelli died four years before it actually happened, worn out from his labors. He had worked in the suppressed Society for more than four decades, the majority of his priestly life.

In August 1814, the monarchs of Europe wept openly at a ceremony where the pope restored the Society of Jesus universally, fulfilling Pignatelli's hopes. Chastened by atheist revolutions and by Napoleon's conquests, these kings and queens repented that their parents had purged the order.

Today, we Jesuits consider St. Joseph Pignatelli to be the second founder of the Society of Jesus. Pope Pius XI described Joseph at his beatification as a priest of "manly and vigorous holiness"; Pope Pius XII later called him the "restorer of the Jesuits." Pius XII canonized St. Joseph Pignatelli in 1954, rewarding his weariness for all eternity.

The Quiet Saint

As a Jesuit, Pope Francis is very familiar with St. Joseph Pignatelli, whom most Catholics do not know. But he is even closer to another little-known Jesuit whom he himself canonized: St. Peter Faber.

Francis announced the "equivalent canonization" for Faber, a rural Savoyard also known as St. Pierre Favre, on his seventy-seventh birthday, December 17, 2013. Although it made few headlines, Francis's birthday gift revealed his deep feeling of kinship with Faber, a priest whose rare gift for spiritual depth in the midst of weariness came from an inner strength rooted in his conviction of Christ's love.

In his fall 2013 interview with Jesuit magazines, the pope had said he admired Faber's "dialogue with all, even the most remote and even with his opponents; his simple piety, a certain naïveté, perhaps; his being available straightaway; his careful interior discernment; the fact that he was a man capable of great and strong decisions but also capable of being so gentle and loving."

Does Faber sound like any other Jesuit we might know?

Acknowledged as a master of prayer and of the *Spiritual Exercises*, Faber had an extraordinary reputation for holiness in his lifetime. People flocked to him for spiritual counsel, including his protégé, St. Peter Canisius — a Dutch Jesuit and later Doctor of the Church who was convinced of Faber's sanctity. St. Francis de Sales, also a Doctor of the Church, likewise knew Faber and spoke of him only as a saint.

But in the centuries after St. Peter Faber died of an illness on his way to the Council of Trent in 1546, Catholics gradually forgot his name. By the time Francis was elected pope, even the most devoted Jesuit groupies were convinced Faber would never be a saint, as they noted the unlikeliness of finding another miracle for a sixteenth-century priest who had been a "blessed" for more than 140 years.

Part of the reason for Faber's obscure reputation was the quiet nature of his personality and work. Although he was one of the first three Jesuits, rooming with St. Ignatius of Loyola and St. Francis Xavier at the University of Paris, Faber rarely said or did anything outwardly extraordinary. Had he not been a cofounder of the Society of Jesus, even later generations of Jesuits might have forgotten him.

A pious young Frenchman, Faber was quietly studying for the diocesan priesthood when Ignatius won his friendship and gave him the *Spiritual Exercises.*

In 1534, when St. Ignatius and his first companions took vows at a chapel in Montmartre, it was Faber — then the only priest among the group — who celebrated the Mass at which they committed themselves to work together for Christ.

Even though his later missions as a Jesuit kept him close to home, Faber spent his priestly life continually on the move, preaching and counseling people from all walks of life. While Loyola started schools and Xavier baptized Japanese pagans, Faber crisscrossed Europe, reforming monasteries and strengthening the faith of wavering Catholics in Reformation Germany.

Working mostly in Protestant-dominated areas, Faber caught more flies with honey than with vinegar, treating non-Catholics with compassion and respect in a way that won admirers to the ancient faith. He mentored future Jesuit St. Francis Borgia and helped establish the Society in Portugal.

There are no popular legends about Faber's ministry, but his humility itself was legendary. Burdened by a scrupulous and quietly intense personality, he leaned on Jesus rather than on himself to overcome temptations to despair. In his spiritual journal, the *Memoriale*, he speaks of the graces he finds and the angels he senses around him as he accompanies God's people on their spiritual journeys.

"Seek grace in the smallest things, and you will find also grace to accomplish, to believe in, and to hope for the greatest things," Faber wrote.

With gentle but powerful gestures, Faber encountered God in spiritual conversations with believers and nonbelievers alike. People found him helpful as a spiritual director, and St. Ignatius declared him to be the best retreat director among the early Jesuits.

In relationships, he was remarkably docile to the Holy Spirit, relaxing his grip on life rather than tightening it during times of stress. Confronted by religious divisions that made many Catholics angry and impatient, he persevered with generosity and openness, empathy and love. To him, Protestants were brothers and sisters in Christ, not demons in disguise.

Like St. Joseph Pignatelli, Faber didn't let anything distract him from his mission to God's people. When louder and flashier missionaries faded away, he continued to lead a quiet life of love. He knew the truth of Jesus' words that "my yoke is easy, and my burden light" (Mt 11:30).

Spiritually, Faber exemplified the Ignatian principle of indifference, or passionate openness to use whatever God gave him in life as a means of salvation. His "Prayer for Detachment," known to Pope Francis and other Jesuits, evokes the strong feelings of a saint who had learned to overcome weariness through a deep consciousness of Jesus Christ's presence in his life:

I beg of you, my Lord,
to remove anything which separates
me from you, and you from me.
Remove anything that makes me unworthy
of your sight, your control, your reprehension;
of your speech and conversation,
of your benevolence and love.
Cast from me every evil
that stands in the way of my seeing you,
hearing, tasting, savoring, and touching you;
fearing and being mindful of you;

knowing, trusting, loving, and possessing you;
being conscious of your presence
and, as far as may be, enjoying you.
This is what I ask for myself
and earnestly desire from you. Amen.

On the day that Faber died at age forty, worn out from his labors, saints and sinners alike wept for him.

Today he is known among Jesuits as "the quiet companion," a priest who preferred the sound of God's voice to the sound of his own. By dispensing with the need for an additional miracle in his canonization decree, Pope Francis essentially declared his entire life to be a miracle.

On August 2, 2014, Francis celebrated St. Peter Faber's feast day with a group of young Jesuit priests, holding up the new saint to them as a model of evangelization. As the pope sees it, missionaries of Faber's mold are not fund-raisers or flashy preachers, but men and women of God who are determined to keep going when the going gets rough. When they reach the point of burnout, they don't throw in the towel, but find a divine presence deep inside of themselves that inspires them to work harder.

For Francis as for Faber, the model of sanctity in weariness is Jesus Christ.

To give and not to count the cost, to toil and not to seek for rest — St. Peter Faber spent each day as if his life depended on these words. And God knows it did.

CHAPTER FIVE

TENDERNESS

Every human being is the object of God's infinite tenderness, and he himself is present in their lives. Jesus offered his precious blood on the cross for that person. Appearances notwithstanding, every person is immensely holy and deserves our love. Consequently, if I can help at least one person to have a better life, that already justifies the offering of my life. (Evangelii Gaudium 274)

I asked the middle-aged man across from me, "Who was the last good American president?"

It was the year 2000. As a nineteen-year-old college journalist studying history and political science, I was eager to know my drinking partner's response to this question. He had just finished railing against Presidents Clinton, Reagan, and Bush 41. At this point, I was wondering if he liked any U.S. president at all.

To my surprise, I didn't have long to wait for an answer. Without hesitation, Christopher Hitchens leaned across the table, looked me in the eye, and quipped with boozy conviction: "Eisenhower." Then he sipped his whiskey, took a drag from his cigarette, and exhaled through his nose as he stared me in the eye, waiting for my reaction amidst the noise of our dingy student hangout.

Amused, I asked, "Why Eisenhower?"

"Because he was the last president who didn't take a dump on the Constitution," Hitchens shot back, taking another drag.

I often think about Hitchens, the British-born journalist who died at sixty-two on December 15, 2011. He had a
knack for punctuating conversations with playful one-liners.
Some of his witticisms still come to mind whenever I go to a
bookstore and see his books on atheism perched — ironically
enough — on the religion and philosophy shelf.

When I shared that drink with him in March 2000, the
self-described "conservative Marxist" had come to Wabash
College in Indiana to debate Ronald Reagan's legacy with the
conservative Catholic political pundit Dinesh D'Souza. It
was Reagan Appreciation Week at Wabash, where the student
news magazine I edited had paid for these two men to cross
swords. (Hitchens later recalled the Wabash debate in an ar-
ticle for Slate.com published on June 7, 2004.)

At the time I saw him debate D'Souza, Hitchens was best
known as a razor-sharp political writer for *The Nation* magazine, not the village atheist he later became. He was different
in those days, more fun and less bitter. I, the future Jesuit, was
not even Catholic when I met him.

Today I marvel at how God brought us together for that
conversation after the debate. In my memory, the Hitchens
who wrote leftist essays for *The Nation* sixteen years ago was
different from the Hitchens who made a public career out of
atheism while dying from esophageal cancer. Sometimes I
wonder whether they were even the same person.

When he visited Wabash sixteen years ago, Hitchens had
written little about God, and was too polite ("I don't want to
offend people," he told me with sincerity) to broach the sub-
ject of religion in the debate. Although he was clearly a disillusioned idealist, he was not unpleasant toward people with
whom he disagreed. He was charming, witty, and friendly to
all the students on our magazine staff. (By contrast, when Bill
Maher did a stand-up comedy routine in the Wabash chapel

in spring 2003, Maher went to great lengths to insult everyone in our small school.)

Despite his high-profile media presence as a writer and TV political pundit, Hitchens was also a more accessible person at the time, keeping his home number listed in the Washington, D.C., telephone book. While interning at *The Washington Times* national desk in 2002, I occasionally called him for comment or background information on stories. He always picked up the phone himself or — if he happened to be at his favorite bar — returned my call within a few hours.

In those days, neither of us knew Hitchens was speaking with a future priest, and we never talked about religion. After he left *The Nation* in 2002, resigning in a feud with his editors over his support for invading Iraq, I never spoke with him again. That same year, I entered the Catholic Church, and he testified against Mother Teresa's cause for sainthood, calling her a "fraud, fanatic, and a fundamentalist."

As I moved closer to God, Hitchens moved further away. Frozen out of Beltway politics by liberals and conservatives alike, he turned more intensely to atheism and the bottle at the same time that I was turning to Mass and the Rosary. Journalist friends told me that Hitchens, well-known around Washington, D.C., as a functional alcoholic, sat at the same bar every day drinking whiskey and nursing his grievances. I suspect it was there that he grew ever more hardened in his belief that God was the cause of all the world's miseries. He advanced this theory in his 2007 best-selling book *God Is Not Great*.

Over the last four years of his life, atheism became his calling card as he allowed his battle with religion to overshadow the rest of his journalistic career. Indeed, Hitchens arguably erased his career as a nonsectarian political writer in the public eye, leaving only his legacy as a public atheist to posterity. If you ask Americans about him today, how many will recall that Hitchens spent most of his career as a political writer rather than as an atheist writer?

I eventually learned that Hitchens had started his career in Britain as an idealistic liberal writer who valued truth in politics, but who frequently ruffled his allies' feathers with his iconoclastic words. As a student radical in the 1960s, he fell out with the Labor Party over its compromise with the Vietnam War. Following his disillusionment with British politics, he moved to the United States, where he was a frequent voice on American talk shows by the mid-1990s.

But in the late 1990s, the Democratic Party abruptly disowned Hitchens when he turned against President Clinton, testifying in an impeachment hearing that Clinton advisor Sidney Blumenthal had told him about a White House campaign to discredit Monica Lewinsky as a "stalker."

It was the beginning of the end for Hitchens in mainstream politics. Yet he continued to maintain an uneasy connection with the American left until 2002, when his support of the Iraq war led to his departure from *The Nation*.

As his disaffection with liberal circles left him without friends in Washington, Hitchens embraced public atheism with a renewed fervor. He emerged in his last years as a popular atheist author for whom God-bashing was now a favorite sport. At the same time, his personal life declined rapidly.

His movement toward public atheism was a sea change in his career. Other than writing a book against Mother Teresa in 1995, Hitchens was simply a political writer when I first met him. He even professed humanitarian concerns in the Wabash debate, telling D'Souza the Reagan administration had funded the rape and torture of American nuns in El Salvador as part of a "campaign of lying and savagery."

He was vain and particular in his habits, smoking mountains of strong Turkish cigarettes which I suspect were more immediately responsible for his esophageal cancer than God.

"The air reeks of smokelessness," he quipped to us after arriving on the Wabash campus. He also joked about Indiana's blue laws concerning liquor, which had somehow prevented him from ordering a second drink one Sunday night at the local Applebee's while his first whiskey was still unfinished.

It's hard to fathom how such a person meets the end of his life. I only know Hitchens suffered a lot in his final illness, and I'm sorry he's gone. When I think of him today, I like to recall him as the quick-witted journalist I met at Wabash, rather than as the conflicted atheist he later became. But I also know they were the same person: a frustrated idealist who was filled with much bitterness despite also being a deeply compassionate man.

God's Tenderness

God loves every human being with infinite tenderness, regardless of whether that person is a believer or a public atheist like Hitchens.

As Pope Francis teaches us, this divine love that restores our dignity and gives us joy is more tender than the love of a father for his children. When we are weary and stumbling, God raises us up. The pope writes:

> Time and time again he bears us on his shoulders. No one can strip us of the dignity bestowed upon us by this boundless and unfailing love. With a tenderness which never disappoints, but is always capable of restoring our joy, he makes it possible for us to lift up our heads and to start anew. (*Evangelii Gaudium* 3)

While Jesus calls us to treat people on the margins tenderly, we may find the need to pray continually to accept this grace, particularly when dealing with people we find challenging. Going out to the margins, we will encounter atheists and people who really do not like us. On such occasions, Francis suggests that it will help our prayer to reflect on the gentle quality of Christ's love for us, before we try to demonstrate it to others.

Although Jesuits hardly own the copyright on tenderness as an image of God's love, there is a distinctively Ignatian style to the pope's emphasis on it.

In one of the warmest prayers attributed to St. Ignatius, the Anima Christi or "Soul of Christ," we ask Jesus Christ to permeate our bodies and souls in an intimate union. Used in the *Spiritual Exercises,* it is a petitionary prayer that Francis and every other Jesuit know well. The usual English translation speaks of an intimate relationship between God and the forgiven sinner:

> Soul of Christ, sanctify me
> Body of Christ, save me
> Blood of Christ, inebriate me
> Water from the side of Christ, wash me
> Passion of Christ, strengthen me
> O Good Jesus, hear me
> Within thy wounds, hide me
> Permit me not to be separated from thee
> From the wicked foe, defend me
> At the hour of my death, call me
> and bid me come to thee
> that with thy angels and saints I may praise thee
> forever and ever.
> Amen.

We invite Jesus closer to us when we ask him to sanctify, save, inebriate, wash, strengthen, hear, hide, defend, and call us. In his own writings, Francis uses the word tenderness a lot to describe this affectionate quality of our relationships to God and neighbor. How does it characterize God's interactions with us? How should it characterize our interactions with others?

Experiencing God

We all experience God's tenderness in different ways, especially through prayer.

As a Jesuit, I've learned some of these ways from giving spiritual direction and directing people on individual retreats. Although we speak to God in prayer, I've learned that our felt experience of his warm response is often more important than the words we use. In particular, I've noticed six ways that people commonly experience God's tenderness in prayer.

For starters, some of us feel God's tenderness most clearly in our experiences of nature. Some people describe their prayer in this kind of language:

> I like to pray when I'm walking around outside. I go
> to the lake or to a park, empty my mind, and start
> tuning in to nature as I walk around. I sense God in
> the sounds of the animals, the feel of the wind, the
> taste of the air, and the smells of the world. I'm awed
> by what God created.

Can we recall a time when we felt God's tenderness in the beauty of creation?

At other times, God comes to us through our feelings. People often talk about their prayer in these kinds of words:

> When I sit down with my Bible to pray in the Ignatian way, I imagine myself as a disciple in the Gospel
> scene that I'm reading, interacting with Jesus. I close
> my eyes and pay attention to what he's like and to
> what I'm seeing, tasting, hearing, saying, smelling,
> touching, and feeling. As I pray in this way, certain
> feelings come up consistently within my heart that I
> know are coming from God. I feel Jesus very near to
> me at these moments.

When was the last time, either in reading Scripture or in interacting with a friend, that we experienced God's tenderness in what we were feeling?

Sometimes God comes to us in desire or touch. People in spiritual direction sometimes report this kind of experience:

> When I was praying over my suffering and imagining Jesus sitting beside me, I suddenly felt Jesus resting his hand on my shoulder, supporting me. Later in church, when I kissed his statue and lit a candle out of my desire to be closer to him in my pain, I sensed him smiling at me.

Can we remember a time when we desired God greatly? Can we remember ever having felt his touch?

We also experience God through others. It's not uncommon for people in spiritual direction to share stories like this one:

> In the hospital last week, our parish priest came to anoint my mother before her surgery. He invited the entire family gathered to lay hands on her and pray silently for a few moments afterward. Suddenly I had this deep sense of God's presence in the members of my family that surprised and comforted me. There was a feeling of God's peaceful nearness in our shared concern that I had never noticed before.

Can we recall God ever revealing himself to us through another person or persons?

Among Catholics, it's also common to experience God's tenderness in our celebration of the sacraments, particularly confession and the Eucharist. In spiritual direction, we often hear this sort of comment:

> After receiving Communion last week, I had a deep feeling of being loved by God, and I decided sponta-

neously to stay for the holy hour after Mass. The feeling of God's love in Communion deepened during this period of silent thanksgiving after Mass.

Can we remember the last time we felt — really felt on a deep level — God's love for us in our reception of a sacrament?

Finally, at certain times in our lives we simply sense that God is near, without feeling any need to analyze it further. People sometimes say:

> God often comes to me when I least expect it. A few days ago, I was praying about a big decision in my life that's been bothering me, and I kept asking him to "show me a sign so I can know what to do." After an hour, I sensed him saying: "My silence is your sign. Wait until you've calmed down before you make a decision." I knew God was with me, and I began to cry.

When was the last time we simply felt God's tender closeness?

This is an important question because in these moments we come closer to the divine love that Pope Francis invites us to share with others.

Christ's Tenderness

When Jesus Christ preaches and heals in the Gospels, the people he meets are amazed by the fact that he teaches "with authority" (see Mt 7:29, Mk 1:22, Lk 4:32) despite being a gentle and unassuming carpenter — a poor worker from a poor town. Throughout the Gospels, Jesus surprises total strangers by the intimate and friendly way he interacts with them.

In the Gospel of John, chapter 4, Jesus astonishes the Samaritan woman at Jacob's well by talking to her casually, even though she is a woman and belongs to a religious splinter group that most Jews despised or avoided. Lulled into talking freely after Jesus asks her for a drink, the woman begins talking about her living situation, only to be shocked when Jesus reveals that he knows she is living with a man outside of wedlock. The amusing exchange occurs in verses 17–18:

> The woman answered and said to him, "I do not have a husband." Jesus answered her, "You are right in saying, 'I do not have a husband.' For you have had five husbands, and the one you have now is not your husband. What you have said is true."

Rather than react with anger or defensiveness in the next verses, this woman seems touched that Jesus knows these facts and shows interest in her. While Jesus' words may seem offensive on the written page, we may assume by the woman's reaction that he spoke them with a tone of affection for her — perhaps even with a little gentle humor. Jesus likes this woman and cares for her.

In verses 23–25, Jesus proceeds to do something even more shocking: He reveals himself as God. Rather than run away, the woman reveals a deep faith hidden by her previous banter. Jesus begins the exchange by telling her of the coming kingdom:

> "But the hour is coming, and is now here, when true worshipers will worship the Father in Spirit and truth; and indeed the Father seeks such people to worship him. God is Spirit, and those who worship him must worship in Spirit and truth." The woman said to him, "I know that the Messiah is coming, the one called the Anointed; when he comes, he will tell us everything." Jesus said to her, "I am he, the one who is speaking with you."

Despite centuries of catechesis, the disarming and unexpected nature of this New Testament passage retains its power for readers today: Jesus Christ, our Lord and Savior, reveals his divinity to a poor and insignificant woman — a sinner who has gone through five husbands and is now living with a man out of wedlock. Jesus didn't have to reveal himself to this woman, but he did so anyway. Far from feeling condemnatory or heavy, this story offers a warm and even joyful picture of Jesus, the man who delights in spending time with people nobody else wants to see.

In Jesus' day, people came from miles around just to see the man who treated ordinary sinners as his friends. Today, many Christians make pilgrimages of their own to get closer to Jesus. One of them is "Pilgrim George" Walter, a Catholic layman from western Pennsylvania who has walked more than forty thousand miles in forty-one countries since 1970.

Walter, dressed in a hand-stitched robe of patched denim, walks hundreds of miles at a time wearing sandals made of Bridgestone tire rubber. Carrying a staff topped with a cross, he often runs across people who question him about what he is doing.

They ask, "Where are you going?"

Walter's response is always succinct: "Heaven!"

Others ask: "What are you doing?"

"Walking for Jesus," Walter replies, smiling.

The bearded and bespectacled pilgrim, who now more frequently resides in a Byzantine Catholic monastery as age prevents him from traveling, often impresses bystanders with his smiling and joyful attitude. He often stops to spend time with strangers who approach him for blessings and conversation.

Wearing an icon of the Madonna and child around his neck, Walter carries a large Bible and a Chotki, Eastern Christian prayer beads on which he repeats the Jesus Prayer — "Lord Jesus Christ, Son of God, have mercy on me, a sinner" — over and over again.

In the course of his many years since he heard the call to spend his life walking on pilgrimage, Walter has met Pope St. John Paul II and many others both important and unimportant. But his sense of Jesus Christ's tender presence and warm love comforts and sustains him on the walk. It is the source of his joy.

More Father than Father

When our relationships between ourselves and others break down, we often find that our relationship with God is the last thing working for us, giving us hope through his tender presence in our lives.

At San Quentin State Prison overlooking San Francisco Bay, I have often given inmates a prayer card with the following quote from Pope Francis:

> God is in everyone's life. Even if the life of a person has been a disaster, even if it is destroyed by vices, drugs or anything else — God is in this person's life. You can — you must — try to seek God in every human life.

Pope Francis reminds us that the God in our lives is more father than any human father, more lover than any lover, and more friend than any friend. He encourages us to open our hearts to Christ, growing ever closer to this presence. That's not always an easy thing to do, particularly when we are sick or in prison, oppressed and suffering.

The Bible offers us various images of God — including father, brother, mother, lover, and friend — to help us reconnect with our Lord when we need him the most. Because God is completely "other," and because we relate to him in a different way than the world — than the people who physically surround us — we cannot say God is quite the same thing as a human father or brother. But when we experience God's loving tenderness, we touch the edges of a supernatural reality that is infinitely more profound than anything we can experience in our earthly lifetimes.

In downtown St. Louis in 1959, a tough-talking Jesuit priest named Fr. Charles Dismas Clark (1902–1963) scrounged the funding to open Dismas House, the nation's first halfway house for homeless ex-convicts. Dedicated to reforming men society had written off, Fr. Clark faced opposition from journalists and law enforcement officials who claimed he was being soft on criminals. Hollywood star Don Murray, impressed by Fr. Clark in a chance meeting, later played the Jesuit in a gritty film called *The Hoodlum Priest* (1961) — a production that Murray partly financed with his own money.

As a young priest in the missions, Fr. Clark had met prisoners in jails and flop houses, mastering their street language and becoming friends with them. Strongly convinced of man's basic goodness, he adopted the middle name "Dismas" in honor of the good thief who died on the cross beside Jesus. Sometimes people who met him believed the priest to be an ex-convict himself because of the slang he used in ordinary conversations — the vocabulary of homeless shelters and chain gangs.

By the time Fr. Clark died in 1963, Dismas House was receiving about five hundred convicts a year and had become a model for future halfway houses in the United States. Some law enforcement officials continued to deride his center as useless. But the ex-convicts who ate and prayed with Fr. Clark each day loved him because he took them seriously and enjoyed spending time with them.

Like Pope Francis, Fr. Clark was convinced that God is in everyone's life. When we see Jesus face to face after our deaths, we will recognize this presence more clearly and feel its tenderness more deeply than anything we ever imagined possible. So will the unbelievers, Samaritans, and thieves who noticed it before us.

Perhaps Christopher Hitchens is already waiting for us in heaven. I certainly hope so.

CHAPTER SIX

MARY

With the Holy Spirit, Mary is always present in the midst of the people. She joined the disciples in praying for the coming of the Holy Spirit (Acts 1:14) and thus made possible the missionary outburst which took place at Pentecost.

She is the Mother of the Church which evangelizes, and without her we could never truly understand the spirit of the new evangelization. (Evangelii Gaudium *284*)

She was nobody — a struggling, illiterate girl from a poor town in the middle of nowhere. She became an unwed pregnant teenager who was on track to give birth to a fatherless baby. But God looked on her with mercy, as he had chosen her to bear his only Son. Today we call her the Mother of God and Mother of the Church, without whose "yes" there would be no Christianity as we know it.

We Catholics may sometimes forget that Mary of Nazareth, the mother of Jesus Christ, was as human as each of us. In our high Mariology, we may even try to soften the crisis pregnancy described in chapter one of the Gospel of Luke by pointing out that Mary was *betrothed* to her future husband Joseph — something more than a modern engagement and yet less than an actual marriage — when she was found with child.

But as far as I'm concerned, the scandal of Mary's pregnancy was actually worse in first-century Palestine than it might be today. Few societies threaten to stone unwed mothers to death in the twenty-first century. We certainly don't execute people for adultery in the United States.

So, betrothed or not, Mary was unmarried and perhaps around fourteen years old according to the marriageable age for women at the time. And she was pregnant.

To make matters worse, her son was eventually arrested as a criminal and executed when he was only thirty-three years old.

Could anyone possibly have felt more excluded from society than this woman?

We Catholics consider Mary the most important saint of our faith for one basic reason: she carried God himself in her body for nine months, being physically united to Jesus Christ in a way that is utterly unique in human history. She was physically closer to God than any other human being has been or will ever be.

She experienced Gospel joy in her encounter with the angel and in her visit to her cousin Elizabeth.

And yet her heart was pierced, broken open, and humbled as a result of her faithful discipleship. Mary lived on the margins of society. She suffered.

Because of these experiences, Pope Francis writes that Mary is the model disciple who goes out to the margins as a missionary of Christ's love:

> Mary was able to turn a stable into a home for Jesus, with poor swaddling clothes and an abundance of love. She is the handmaid of the Father who sings his praises. She is the friend who is ever concerned that wine not be lacking in our lives. She is the woman whose heart was pierced by a sword and who understands all our pain.
>
> As mother of all, she is a sign of hope for peoples suffering the birth pangs of justice. She is the missionary who draws near to us and accompanies us throughout life, opening our hearts to faith by her maternal love. As a true mother, she walks at our side,

she shares our struggles and she constantly surrounds us with God's love. (*Evangelii Gaudium* 286)

It's precisely for these reasons that Pope Francis invites us to pray to Mary as mother of evangelization: She understands firsthand, better than anyone else, how to relate to people on the margins who most need God's love. She received Christ's love in her own brokenness before the rest of us ever knew him.

Being attentive to the foundational reality of Mary's story can give us a starting-point for theologizing about her role in our lives as we go out to the margins. Far from an academic task, Francis notes that even ordinary people begin to theologize when they turn to Mary in their need. He writes:

> I think of the steadfast faith of those mothers tending their sick children who, though perhaps barely familiar with the articles of the creed, cling to a rosary; or of all the hope poured into a candle lighted in a humble home with a prayer for help from Mary, or in the gaze of tender love directed to Christ crucified.
>
> No one who loves God's holy people will view these actions as the expression of a purely human search for the divine. They are the manifestation of a theological life nourished by the working of the Holy Spirit who has been poured into our hearts (cf. Rom 5:5). (*Evangelii Gaudium* 125)

Francis, who grew up attending Marian devotions with his Grandmother Rosa, understands how Mary brings experience and theology together in our lives. When we go to people on the margins, we often find Mary there as well as her son. As the ideal disciple, Mary models the joy, longing, closeness, dignity, weariness, and tenderness that we have been discussing in this book as a call from Jesus Christ to go out to the margins.

And there is deep theological significance in the way Francis talks about Mary. By viewing Mary as Mother of the Church that evangelizes, the pope is taking a page from Vatican II. In *Lumen Gentium*, chapter eight, the Second Vatican Council called Mary "the symbol of the Church" — noting that she represents the community and individual believers alike.

In recent years, Catholic theologians have worked to articulate an anthropological (human-centered) view of Mary that complements our Church's dogmas about her. Rather than seek to formulate new Marian dogmas, they have made renewed efforts to understand Mary as a human being. As Pope Francis does, we may find it helpful ourselves to reflect on how Mary shares our humanity, bringing us ever closer to her Son on the margins.

Being Attentive to Mary's Humanity

To probe the full range of Mary's saga in the biblical infancy narratives, we must consider it prior to the Bible's theological interpretation of it, recovering the *human experiences* of the underlying historical events.

Cardinal Avery Dulles, S.J., described the Bible as "interpreted history." As such, before we try to help marginalized people understand Marian dogmas, we will do well to be attentive to the existential reality that led Mary to say "yes" to God. For as Pope Francis insists, it is Mary's experience of God's call that makes her such a strong model for our missionary response to Christ.

So where do we begin?

Quests for the historical Jesus aside, the infancy narratives of St. Luke and St. Matthew remain our primary source for information about Mary's pregnancy and motherhood.

In these Gospel accounts of Mary's motherhood of Jesus, God's only Son who is also God himself, we find the basis of

Mariology's most essential teaching that Mary is the *Theotokos*, or Mother of God. This dogma is the source from which all other Marian dogmas, including the Immaculate Conception, flow in their historical development.

Curiously, the Bible gives us two different windows on the same reality: Matthew tells the story of Mary's pregnancy from Joseph's perspective, while Luke tells it from the viewpoint of Mary.

Matthew's Gospel, after opening with a genealogy emphasizing Jesus' descent from Abraham and David, confronts us with an unsettling image from the male perspective that no royal lineage can soften: a man named Joseph confronts his future bride, who is pregnant, and he knows he isn't the father because he and his betrothed have not slept together.

In this first book of the New Testament, our first image of Mary in Scripture thus seems to be the most unsettling and existentially accurate: Mary stands before her promised husband — and the reader — as an unwed pregnant teenager.

I have already mentioned how Mary's betrothal to Joseph, a more serious commitment in ancient Jewish culture than a modern wedding engagement, doesn't disguise the fact that her son appears in Matthew's narrative as illegitimate. If anything, it makes matters worse, as Joseph resolves to send his betrothed away to save her (and Jesus in the womb) from the death penalty commanded by the Law of Moses for adulterers. So instead of the death penalty he offers Mary the relatively honorable alternative (in that culture) of suffering in destitution as an unwed mother excluded from society.

Only the angel's subsequent appearance to *Joseph* — there is no apparition to Mary in Matthew's Gospel — stops this plan and persuades the carpenter to take Mary into his home as his wife. The human dimension of this confrontation between Joseph and Mary is brilliantly visualized in Pier Paolo

Pasolini's film masterpiece *The Gospel According to Matthew* (1964), a classic of Italian neorealist cinema.

Pasolini, an atheist Marxist and homosexual who felt inspired by Pope St. John XXIII to visualize the human side of Christ's life, makes the creative choice to skip the genealogy of Matthew, chapter one — and indeed all the "narrated" text of Matthew — to utilize only the Gospel's dialogue in his film.

Stripped of Matthew's theological narration of Mary's experience, the now-wordless scene of Joseph finding Mary with child opens the movie with a visceral realism that feels almost like a silent film: Pasolini gives us close-ups of Joseph's face, Mary's face, and then long camera shots which "show" rather than "tell" us what is happening between them.

The first thing we see is Mary's face, suffused in guarded innocence and trusting humility. Visually, Pasolini's next two shots communicate that she has just told Joseph she is pregnant, giving us a close-up of his shocked face and a long shot of her pregnant belly.

Joseph's face, in a brilliant series of camera shots, is intensely ambiguous: Feelings of surprise, doubt, anguish, and even anger appear to flicker across his face as he finally paces back and forth. Joseph looks so upset that he needs to walk away to make sure he doesn't say or do something he will regret. In the next scene, the angel appears as Joseph puts his head down to rest, speaking the movie's first words in regard to accepting Mary and her child into his home.

Following Catholic tradition, Pasolini shows us a Mary who looks fifteen years old and an older Joseph around thirty, both dressed in rags and surrounded by the unfeigned poverty of the Italian slum where the movie was made — a location strongly evocative of the margins Pope Francis now preaches about.

Artistically, Pasolini's film suggests an image of Mary's humanity that precedes all theological reflection, including the theology of the Gospel writer himself. This Mary is no regal queen descended from David, nor an otherworldly being come from God, but a poor girl in a forgotten town who appears secure in the knowledge of her virtue despite the inexplicable nature of her pregnancy.

Throughout the rest of the film, Pasolini casts homeless people and laborers in key roles, showing us lots of toothless grins and other trappings of the reality to which Christ calls us as missionaries. As the older Mary at the crucifixion, he casts his own weary-looking mother.

While some scholars date Luke's Gospel earlier than the Gospel of Matthew, the unvarnished humanity of Matthew's account of Mary's pregnancy — disrupted only by the angel's subsequent appearance to reassure Joseph of his wife's innocence — suggests to me that it might date from an earlier oral tradition than the annunciation of Luke.

Unlike Matthew, Luke opens his Gospel from the female perspective (Elizabeth and Mary) after a brief explanatory prelude. Here we find the parallel birth narratives of John the Baptist and Jesus which are familiar to Christian popular piety and secular Christmas card shoppers.

The miraculous conception of John by Zechariah and his barren wife Elizabeth, who is Mary's cousin, prefigures the next scene where the Angel Gabriel announces a miraculous pregnancy to Mary, who says "yes" to God despite protesting her virginity.

Although Luke's account feels more heavily theologized than Matthew's narrative, we sense here the underlying human core of an unwed virgin teenager who surrenders to the mystery of her reality after experiencing divine reassurance that her inexplicable pregnancy is from God. Luke gives us the image of a young virgin girl who, through divine insight, interprets her crisis pregnancy as a gift from God. In Luke's narrative, we read the story through Mary's eyes rather than through Joseph's, shifting the perspective away from Matthew's emphasis.

Another Italian filmmaker, Franco Zeffirelli, echoes Pasolini's raw take on Matthew by reimagining Luke's annunciation scene in his English-language film *Jesus of Nazareth* (1977) from a strongly humanistic perspective. As her worried mother looks on, Mary (Olivia Hussey) kneels before the moonlight streaming through the window of her room, but we see and hear only her side of the biblical conversation with the angel.

By declining to visualize or voice the angel, this psychological depiction of Mary's experience focuses squarely on her human emotional responses of fear and trusting surrender. It emphasizes Mary's humanity without overly spiritualizing her "yes" *(fiat)* to God or limiting her divine encounter to the most literal interpretation.

Like all great art, the Jesus films of Pasolini and Zeffirelli can help us get beneath the theological varnish of Mary's pregnancy in the infancy narratives, exposing the underlying core of a frightened virgin girl and her future husband responding to an inexplicable pregnancy. The late Jesuit theologian Karl Rahner might have described their behavior as "surrendering to the mystery" of Mary's encounter with God, accepting the grace of what the Church later defined as her divine motherhood.

Pope Francis and Mary

To pray to Mary as mother implies a sophisticated theology among even the simplest believers. Recognizing her as the mother of all believers, Francis describes Mary as Christ's gift of guidance and comfort to the Church:

> Jesus left us his mother to be our mother. Only after doing so did Jesus know that "all was now finished"

(Jn 19:28). At the foot of the cross, at the supreme hour of the new creation, Christ led us to Mary. He brought us to her because he did not want us to journey without a mother, and our people read in this maternal image all the mysteries of the Gospel. The Lord did not want to leave the Church without this icon of womanhood. (*Evangelii Gaudium* 285)

In this view, to read "all the mysteries of the Gospel" in our maternal image of Mary does not represent a superstitious or anti-intellectual form of religious faith. Rather, it is an attempt to do a theology that is incarnated in people's everyday experiences.

On our daily journey to God, Francis sees Mary as a model of joyful gratitude that helps us preach the Gospel effectively. He writes:

The memory of the faithful, like that of Mary, should overflow with the wondrous things done by God. Their hearts, growing in hope from the joyful and practical exercise of the love which they have received, will sense that each word of Scripture is a gift before it is a demand. (*Evangelii Gaudium* 142)

As with all things, our connection to God's maternal love that we find symbolized in Mary begins with prayer. Pope Francis himself prefers an obscure German devotion to the Mother of God under the patronage of "Mary, Undoer of Knots."

Francis discovered this devotion while he was on a sabbatical in Germany to work on an advanced degree in theology. Although he ultimately decided not to finish the degree, he picked up the devotion and made it a part of his prayer life.

The Baroque painting of this devotion, which shows Mary patiently untying a badly knotted rope with the assistance of two angels, conveys a simple message: When our lives get all tangled up through sin and other obstacles, we can trust the Blessed Mother to help us unravel the knots.

Mary on the Margins

The Bible gives us many stories of Mary that illustrate the themes of this book's earlier chapters.

We see Mary experience joy at the birth of her son. She expresses her longing for God in the "yes" of her annunciation, her closeness to her Son in protecting him from Herod, and her dignity as a mother in walking with Christ to his humiliating death.

Mary experiences weariness when the twelve-year-old Jesus stays behind in the Temple during a family trip, obliging her to search for him with great worry. She feels tenderness in caring for Jesus and his disciples.

But this Mother of Evangelization plays a more immediate role for Pope Francis: When we go to the needy as missionaries, we find Mary waiting for us there.

Throughout history, Mary has been close to the experiences of the poor and marginalized, particularly through her reported apparitions. She shows a special care for ordinary human beings.

In 1531, St. Juan Diego reported that Mary appeared to him in the hills of Tepeyac near Mexico City, bringing a message of hope and comfort. The indigenous image of Our Lady of Guadalupe that Juan — himself an illiterate Indian — brought back with him mysteriously imprinted on his tilma, or cloak, continues to resound with the powerless in Latin America and beyond.

Cesar Chavez carried images of Guadalupe in his United Farmworkers protests of the 1960s. And not too many years ago, a beauty pageant contestant in Mexico wore a designer dress covered with images of Guadalupe.

At Our Lady of Guadalupe Jesuit parish in San Antonio, Texas, a local beauty pageant queen even donated her crown to the parish's patroness in 2011. Domonique Ramirez, the city's seventeen-year-old "Miss San Antonio" winner, surprised the pastor (Fr. Ron Gonzales, S.J.) by entering the church one day with an entourage. Praying briefly before the image of Guadalupe, she placed the crown on the altar as a gift to Mary.

"She's the queen of all queens, the keeper of all crowns. I wanted to give my crown to her," Ramirez told the local press.

Like her son, Jesus, the Mother of God seems to pop up everywhere. On February 11, 1858, Mary appeared to fourteen-year-old Bernadette Soubirous, an illiterate peasant girl in the southern French town of Lourdes. Bernadette, gathering firewood near the city dump one day, said Mary gave her messages and asked her to dig up a spring in the ground.

After miraculous healings began occurring at this spring, located in a grotto of the dump, Our Lady of Lourdes became an instant sensation. Today Lourdes is one of the largest Christian pilgrimage sites in the world, receiving millions of visitors each year who come in search of physical and spiritual healing. Marginalized and sick people feel Mary's presence at Lourdes. Not far away, the incorrupt body of St. Bernadette lies beneath glass in a small chapel at the convent where she lived out her final years as a nun.

In almost all cases of reported Marian apparitions, the visionaries are poor and needy, not rich and powerful. While Catholics aren't required to believe in these apparitions as part of the faith revealed by Christ, the sites of these events have become places of encounter with God for millions of ordinary believers throughout the world.

From May 13 to October 13, 1917, Mary reportedly appeared to three shepherd children in the Portuguese village of Fátima. As Europe was imploding all around them in the

Great War, the three children said Our Lady of Fátima asked them for prayers to stop people from sinning. Fátima soon became another international pilgrimage site that continues to draw visitors today.

Pilgrims to Fátima have included popes as well as paupers. When Pope John Paul II was shot at point-blank range by a hit man on May 13, 1981, he attributed his miraculous survival to Our Lady of Fátima — the shooting had occurred on the anniversary of her first apparition to the children.

Traveling to Fátima after his recovery to thank Mary for his life, John Paul II approached a statue of the Blessed Mother and placed the bullet that was recovered from the assassination attempt inside the crown atop her head.

Like Pope St. John Paul II, Pope Francis appreciates Mary's concern for the poor and needy. He also promotes the Marian prayer devotions which have brought comfort to millions of people on the margins throughout the centuries.

Marian Devotions

As a Jesuit, Francis has a particular spiritual bond to Mary. Like all members of the Society of Jesus, Francis professed his first vows "in the presence of the Virgin Mother, the whole heavenly court, and all those here present...." He later did the same when he professed his final vows of poverty, chastity, obedience, and the special "fourth vow" of Jesuit obedience to the pope.

Nevertheless, the Holy Father's personal devotion to Mary runs deeper than his religious vows and retreat experiences, being an active part of his daily life. Francis is an enthusiastic fan of the Rosary, spiritual reading, and other devotional practices centered on Mary and the saints — including St. Joseph, whose name the pope has inserted into more of the Eucharistic prayers at Mass. Francis writes:

Genuine forms of popular religiosity are incarnate, since they are born of the incarnation of Christian faith in popular culture. For this reason they entail a personal relationship, not with vague spiritual energies or powers, but with God, with Christ, with Mary, with the saints. These devotions are fleshy, they have a face. They are capable of fostering relationships and not just enabling escapism. (*Evangelii Gaudium* 90)

Once again, Francis insists on the earthy reality of Mary and Christ, prayer and devotion. He is not talking about escapist metaphors when he speaks of these things, but of relational realities. When we ask Mary's intercession as "star of evangelization," Francis likewise insists, we may do so confidently in the hope that she will take our prayers to God.

The pope concludes *The Joy of the Gospel* with an exhortation and prayer to Mary as the model of our evangelization to people on the margins. Although lengthy, it is worth quoting in full.

There is a Marian "style" to the Church's work of evangelization. Whenever we look to Mary, we come to believe once again in the revolutionary nature of love and tenderness. In her we see that humility and tenderness are not virtues of the weak but of the strong who need not treat others poorly in order to feel important themselves.

Contemplating Mary, we realize that she who praised God for "bringing down the mighty from their thrones" and "sending the rich away empty" (Lk 1:52–53) is also the one who brings a homely warmth to our pursuit of justice. She is also the one who carefully keeps "all these things, pondering them in her heart" (Lk 2:19).

Mary is able to recognize the traces of God's Spirit in events great and small. She constantly contemplates the mystery of God in our world, in human history and in our daily lives. She is the woman of prayer and work in Nazareth, and she is also Our Lady of Help, who sets out from her town "with haste" (Lk 1:39) to be of service to others.

This interplay of justice and tenderness, of contemplation and concern for others, is what makes the ecclesial community look to Mary as a model of evangelization. We implore her maternal intercession that the Church may become a home for many peoples, a mother for all peoples, and that the way may be opened to the birth of a new world. It is the Risen Christ who tells us, with a power that fills us with confidence and unshakeable hope: "Behold, I make all things new" (Rev 21:5). With Mary we advance confidently towards the fulfillment of this promise, and to her we pray:

> Mary, Virgin and Mother,
> you who, moved by the Holy Spirit,
> welcomed the word of life
> in the depths of your humble faith:
> as you gave yourself completely to the
>   Eternal One,
> help us to say our own "yes"
> to the urgent call, as pressing as ever,
> to proclaim the good news of Jesus.

> Filled with Christ's presence,
> you brought joy to John the Baptist,
> making him exult in the womb of his mother.
> Brimming over with joy,
> you sang of the great things done by God.
> Standing at the foot of the cross
> with unyielding faith,
> you received the joyful comfort of the
>   resurrection,
> and joined the disciples in awaiting the Spirit
> so that the evangelizing Church might be born.

Obtain for us now a new ardor born
    of the resurrection,
that we may bring to all the Gospel of life
which triumphs over death.
Give us a holy courage to seek new paths,
that the gift of unfading beauty
may reach every man and woman.

Virgin of listening and contemplation,
Mother of love, Bride of the eternal
    wedding feast,
pray for the Church, whose pure icon you are,
that she may never be closed in on herself
or lose her passion for establishing
    God's kingdom.

Star of the new evangelization,
help us to bear radiant witness to communion,
service, ardent and generous faith,
justice and love of the poor,
that the joy of the Gospel
may reach to the ends of the earth,
illuminating even the fringes of our world.

Mother of the living Gospel,
wellspring of happiness for God's little ones,
pray for us.

Amen. Alleluia! (*Evangelii Gaudium* 288)

Together with all of our actions on God's behalf, what better thing can we ultimately do for evangelization other than pray? After all, we are not God.

And yet we know someone who is pretty close to him. She was poor and needy like us, but God chose her for great things.

As Mary reminds us, God has great desires for each and every one of us.

COURAGE

*Give us a holy courage to seek new paths, that the gift
of unfading beauty may reach every man and woman.*
(Evangelii Gaudium *288*)

It wasn't supposed to end this way.

As he faced the possibility of life with a mutilated leg, the
Spanish captain grimaced in pain, asking the doctors to break
his improperly healed bones and reset them in order to stretch
the limb again.

The battle hadn't gone the way he had planned, but he
had no intention of quitting now.

Íñigo López de Loyola, age thirty, had just returned home
from Pamplona, where an enemy shell had smashed into his
legs, breaking one. After he fell, the Spanish surrendered the
city to its French besiegers.

Enemy doctors had set his leg out of respect and sent
him home to Loyola in Azpeitia, the Basque region of Spain,
but the captain was horrified at what he discovered after getting back there: One leg was shorter than the other because
the bones had healed over each other, creating an ugly lump
of flesh and bone that protruded from his body.

Either the doctors had botched the surgery, or the journey home had jostled his limb while it was healing, or pieces
of his bone fragments had forever been lost on the battlefield.
But none of this mattered to López. After his family physi-
cians inspected the wound, which had completely healed, he
simply told them to break the leg and set the bones again.
They did. It was still shorter than the other one.

At this point, the captain asked his family doctors to start stretching the limb with enormous weights to make it the same length as the other one.

It was the sixteenth century. Without any anesthetics, the doctors did as López asked, and he put up with the pain without uttering a cry. He did so for only one reason, which he kept in mind to distract himself from the agony: to fit into his tight-fitting leather boots again.

As a young courtier and self-appointed knight, López was accustomed to wearing the finest clothing, adorning himself in close-fitting hose underneath a ruffled shirt and a hat with a feather on top. He also wore expensive leather boots that were in fashion at Spain's royal court. There was nothing to live for if he couldn't wear these things again.

In childhood, López's father had sent him to a nobleman's court to be trained as a scribe, but the young *hidalgo* wanted more from life. Spain was the world's leading power, and he dreamed of becoming an important figure in its empire.

He loved to read chivalric romances like *Amadis de Gaul*, the sixteenth-century equivalents of drugstore adventure novels. He dreamed of doing great deeds for Spain, acquiring kingdoms and winning the hands of fair ladies.

But in the real world he grew up to be a womanizer, gambler, and brawler who started duels with anyone who looked at him funny. Once he was jailed for beating up a priest who owed money to his brother, who was also a priest. He got off on a technicality.

To go through life with one lumpy leg shorter than the other meant that he could never fit into that clothing — or into that lifestyle — again. It meant the death of his youthful fantasies.

On the night before his fateful wound, the governor of Pamplona had wanted to surrender immediately to the French, who vastly outnumbered the town's garrison. But Captain López had argued him out of it, extolling the honor of Spain and rallying his few hundred men to the defense.

When the French woke up the next morning to the Spanish flag still flying above Pamplona, they were unimpressed. They shrugged their shoulders and unlimbered their cannons. After a few hours of bombardment, French cannonballs breached the walls. In the breach stood Captain López, his sword drawn, defying the enemy to come at him. He wasn't there long before the cannonball smashed into his legs, sending him to the ground like a sack of potatoes.

The Spanish surrendered almost immediately. Their leader had fallen.

On Death's Door

Back in his family's small castle at Loyola, Captain López passed out from the barbaric surgeries he ordered for himself. His doctor gave him a fifty-fifty chance of surviving until morning. A priest gave him the Last Rites.

Raised as a Catholic, the good soldier had attended Mass twice yearly throughout his life and knew a handful of prayers, mostly because everyone in Spain had the same background. His faith was externally pious, according to the fashion of the royal court, but not deeply felt.

Since he had some devotion to St. Peter, López prayed to the apostle as he was losing consciousness. Peter heard his prayers, and he woke up alive the next morning — as much to his own surprise as to that of his doctors.

Now stuck in bed for ten months of agonizing recovery, he had nothing to do but stare at the walls and think. There was of course no television, phone, or radio.

Eager to keep his mind occupied, the wounded captain asked for books of chivalry to lift his depression, but the family could only find two volumes in the entire house: *Life of Christ* by Ludolph of Saxony and *Readings of the Saints (The Golden Legend)* by Jacobus de Voragine.

López was so bored that he was willing to read anything. He began leafing through the hefty volumes, unenthusiastically at first. But as he read each page with growing interest, something changed within him. He read about Jesus Christ healing the sick, about the great saints like Francis and Dominic preaching to the poor.

When he read these things, it felt like a sword had pierced his heart. Here, for the first time, he was reading about men who had lived their lives for others. And what was López living for? His boots.

Reflecting on his past life, he felt a growing dissatisfaction. Like many young adults, he began to think about the future and to wonder where he would be in a few years. Back in the army, throwing himself in front of another cannonball? For what?

As the youngest of eleven children, he had always worked harder than others to prove himself in the world, but what was it all for?

Feeling inspired by Jesus and the great saints he read about, Íñigo López began to alarm his family, now headed by his older brother Martin since the death of their father. They could see an unnatural gleam in his eyes that bothered them.

When Íñigo was healthy enough to walk, Martin took him on a tour of the castle, pointing to all of the beautiful things in each room. "This is all yours," he told his little brother, "so why throw it away?" He added something along these lines: "I don't know what you're thinking, but I can see that crazy look in your eyes, so don't do it!"

In the midst of the broken soldier's pain and confusion, only one thing made sense: Íñigo wanted to be as close to Jesus

Christ as possible. He wanted it so badly that he could hardly think of anything else.

Having read that many of the great saints went on pilgrimage to Jerusalem, Íñigo decided to do the same. He left home, went to the Duke of Nájera, who served as his superior, and resigned his commission in the army despite the duke's offers of money and promotion to keep him.

After sending home his brother's mule and servant, the captain took a staff and began walking to Jerusalem — from Spain! He wasn't thinking clearly.

But he stopped first at Our Lady of Montserrat, a Benedictine abbey situated high upon a sheer mountain cliff, to dedicate his life to God. There he spent the night in a medieval Vigil of Arms, sometimes standing and sometimes kneeling in prayer before the Black Madonna — an African depiction of Mary left behind from the Muslim conquest of Spain.

In the morning, he left his sword and dagger at the altar, and walked out to the entrance of the church. There he gave all of his clothing to a beggar — his hat with the feather, his ruffled shirt, and his boots.

Then he donned a rough potato sack and took up a walking stick to continue his journey.

But he stopped a second time in Manresa, staying with the Dominicans and going to a little cave on the banks of the Cardoner River to pray every day for ten months.

In the cave he reflected on a journal where he had jotted down notes on the life of Christ from his book. Imagining himself present with the Lord, he immersed himself in the scenes of the Gospels and paid attention to the thoughts and feelings that arose within him. Some of them seemed to come from God and others from the Evil Spirit.

Gradually, he discerned that God was calling him to continue on his path to Jerusalem, and he later published the notes he kept on these prayer experiences in a book called

the *Spiritual Exercises* — to help others on their own journeys to God.

Struggling with scrupulosity over the sins of his past life,
he had inflicted long fasts and severe penances on himself,
allowing his hair and fingernails to grow wildly as his body
wasted away. But now he realized that the better penance was
to serve others out of love for God rather than to punish his
own body.

In Jerusalem, he lingered over the tourist sites of Christ's
life with deep emotion, particularly the Mount of the Ascen-
sion.

Because of fighting in the Holy Land, his trip was cut
short, and he returned to Spain where he began preaching
God's word in the streets and sleeping with the homeless. He
was jailed by the Inquisition, who suspected him during this
Reformation period of being an *alumbrado,* a member of a
mistrusted Spanish mystical movement who denied the sacraments in favor of inner experience. He was eventually acquit-
ted.

A New Path

Realizing he needed an education to dedicate himself to God
publicly, Íñigo studied at Alcala and Salamanca, but decided
after his tangles with the Spanish Inquisition to leave Spain.

He finally ended up at the University of Paris as a forty-
year-old college student with two roommates in their twenties
whom he helped to become saints: Francis Xavier and Peter
Faber. There, he gradually acquired influence over these men
and others, gathering a small circle of wealthy young men who
made his *Spiritual Exercises* and went with him to care for the
sick and dying. He changed his name to Ignatius, paralleling
his change of life.

After earning their master's degrees in philosophy, Ignatius's little group of friends wanted to spend their lives praying in the Holy Land, but war prevented them. So they chose to put themselves at the service of Pope Paul III, who established them as a missionary order called the Society of Jesus that would eventually span the globe in its educational and pastoral reach. He approved the order in 1540.

The "Jesuits" of this order, so-called by those who mocked their unprecedented boldness in choosing the name Jesus for their congregation, grew quickly.

Ignatius spent the rest of his life in Rome, overseeing the growth of his new order and starting a home for reformed prostitutes as well as caring for others in the city's streets. After he died on July 31, 1556, at the age of sixty-five, the Catholic Church made him a saint, celebrating his feast day on the same date. Today he is known in history books as a figure of the Counter-Reformation, a man who sent men all over the globe to evangelize.

But for we who are Jesuits, St. Ignatius of Loyola will always be the broken soldier who entrusted his life to Jesus because he was too humbled to be proud anymore.

Pope Francis and St. Ignatius

It was supposed to end differently.

Like St. Ignatius, Pope Francis found himself led by God on a new path he didn't choose for himself. In March 2013 he was ready to retire. He became pope instead.

As Francis understands it, God chose him out of mercy to be pope, inviting him to share God's mercy with the world.

In the Society of Jesus, every Jesuit's life mirrors the biography of St. Ignatius to some extent, as our formation and way of proceeding follows the sixteenth-century pattern set by our founder and his first companions. It is a life of obedience and of radical availability for mission.

With Pope Francis, the first Jesuit pope, we might consider one point of similarity in particular: Both he and Ignatius were called to finish their apostolic lives in ministries they didn't pursue, but which they accepted as God's will.

If there is any experience that all Jesuits share in common with Ignatius, it is the experience of not getting what we want, and more particularly of getting an assignment different from what we might have chosen for ourselves. Obedience is the primary Jesuit vow. Francis is no exception.

St. Ignatius of Loyola established the mold. Although he set out to live and die as a penitent in the Holy Land evangelizing the Muslim Turks, he found himself obliged by his companions to become the first superior general of the Society of Jesus when his first plan didn't work out. The Society of Jesus, for him, was "Plan B."

Father General Ignatius, rather than going as a missionary to the East, spent the last twenty years of his life working from a desk in Rome — signing real estate transactions, writing spiritual letters and documents for his new order, and generally striving to incarnate his charism for future generations of Jesuits.

Deprived of his dream of evangelizing the Turks, Ignatius had to settle for living vicariously through St. Francis Xavier and the other early Jesuit missionaries he sent out into the Lord's vineyard.

Jorge Mario Bergoglio, who foresaw a simple retirement to obscurity in Argentina, likewise never wanted to be pope. When Pope Benedict XVI resigned, Bergoglio was already one year beyond the retirement age for a cardinal and was waiting for the pope to accept his resignation letter.

Like St. Ignatius, Pope Francis had wanted to be a missionary himself. As a young Jesuit, he even wrote to Father

General Pedro Arrupe asking if he could go to the missions, but Arrupe told him to stay put. And in the end, the wannabe missionary became pope instead — ironically making Jorge Bergoglio a bigger missionary than he ever dreamed possible.

Francis, now working well beyond retirement age, finds himself trying to lead the Catholic Church to the margins in a critical moment of world history that St. Ignatius could never have foreseen.

Yet Francis, the good Jesuit soldier formed by his religious vow of obedience, remains committed to performing his Petrine ministry as far as his abilities will take him. Not for himself, but because the Church — or Christ through the Church — asked him.

Because he senses that God chose him to be pope, rather than that he chose it for himself, Francis feels truly free — free to be himself in loving and serving God wherever divine grace leads him.

Such interior freedom is a hallmark of indifference, that general willingness to use or not use our earthly gifts as they contribute to the greater glory of God — *Ad Majorem Dei Gloriam*. St. Ignatius expressed this ideal of indifference in his First Principle and Foundation that opens the *Spiritual Exercises*:

> Man is created to praise, reverence, and serve God our Lord, and by this means to save his soul.
>
> The other things on the face of the earth are created for man to help him in attaining the end for which he is created.
>
> Hence, man is to make use of them in as far as they help him in the attainment of his end, and he must rid himself of them in as far as they prove a hindrance to him.
>
> Therefore, we must make ourselves indifferent to all created things, as far as we are allowed free choice

and are not under any prohibition. Consequently, as far as we are concerned, we should not prefer health to sickness, riches to poverty, honor to dishonor, a long life to a short life. The same holds for all other things.

Our one desire and choice should be what is more conducive to the end for which we are created. (*The Spiritual Exercises of St. Ignatius*, #23, translated by Louis J. Puhl, S.J.)

As a man of the *Spiritual Exercises*, Francis strives to embody this courageous ideal in his ministry as pope, promoting disinterested love as an ongoing goal for Catholic missionaries in the twenty-first century.

In a world that divinizes self-interest, Francis encourages healthy and compassionate self-sacrifice. Among people who value riches, honors, and pride, he promotes Gospel humility.

Above all else, Francis encourages us to go forward with holy boldness, courageous in the face of worldly trials.

If we are to live out the ideals of *The Joy of the Gospel* as we move further into this century, one fact seems especially relevant — and one needn't be a Jesuit to appreciate it. It is that the answer to all of our deepest human needs is Jesus Christ, embodied in the Catholic Church he founded and continues to sustain today.

To grasp this truth is to grasp everything that matters in life. It is to grasp the only secure anchor on which we can confidently base a missionary commitment to spreading the Gospel in our world today.

At the end of an early meditation from the *Spiritual Exercises*, St. Ignatius poses three questions that Pope Francis and every other Jesuit have prayed over many times. But they are questions for all Christians to ponder. These three questions conclude a "colloquy," or conversation, that Ignatius asks us to have in our imagination:

Imagine Christ our Lord present before you upon the cross, and begin to speak with him, asking how it is that though He is the Creator, He has stooped to become man, and to pass from eternal life to death here in time, that thus He might die for our sins.

I shall also reflect upon myself and ask:

> "What have I done for Christ?"
> "What am I doing for Christ?"
> "What ought I to do for Christ?"

As I behold Christ in this plight, nailed to the cross, I shall ponder upon what presents itself to my mind. (*The Spiritual Exercises of St. Ignatius* #53)

Francis, like his religious father and the other great heroes of our faith, merely points the way to the Savior who stands ready to receive all of us in mercy. For if we do not believe that Jesus Christ rose from the dead, in the physical and bodily sense meant by the Greek verb in our Bible, St. Paul says our faith is in vain. But we must act on this belief in order for it to bear fruit in this world, particularly for those who are in need.

Jesus Christ rose from the dead. Our Redeemer lives. He loves us and calls us as baptized Christians, in love, to love the lonely, the difficult, the hostile, the neglected, the poor, and all the people that no one else wants to love. This good news fills our hearts with joy.

So what are we going to do about it?

What would Pope Francis do?